Preaching That Engages the Whole Congregation

SO THAT ALL MIGHT KNOW

Thomas H. Troeger *and*
H. Edward Everding, Jr.

Abingdo
Nash

SO THAT ALL MIGHT KNOW
PREACHING THAT ENGAGES THE WHOLE CONGREGATION

This book is printed on acid-free paper.

Library of Congress Cataloging-in-Publication Data

Troeger, Thomas H., 1945–
    So that all might know : preaching that engages the whole congregation / Thomas H. Troeger, H. Edward Everding, Jr.
        p.cm.
    ISBN 978-0-687-65238-9 (pbk. : alk. paper)
    1. Preaching—Psychology. 2. Multiple intelligences—Religious aspects—Christianity. I. Everding, H. Edward. II. Title.

    BV4235.P79T76 2008
    251.001'9—dc22

                                                        2007050829

08 09 10 11 12 13 14 15 16 17—10 9 8 7 6 5 4 3 2 1
MANUFACTURED IN THE UNITED STATES OF AMERICA

To the memory of Henry,
whose life revealed the wonder of
human knowing,
and
in gratitude to our students,
who embody that wonder in their
lives

More Praise for So That All Might Know:

"One of the gifts of this book is that it assumes children are present in worship and addresses their perspectives on religious concepts along with identifying the different ways adults approach the world. Sermon examples help pastors see how the theories apply in practice."
> —**Kathy Black,** Professor of Homiletics and Liturgics, Claremont School of Theology

"Can a preacher find a language that can truly be heard by everyone? Basing their study on the theory of multiple intelligences, Troeger and Everding offer a lively homiletic characterized by humble attention to the real ears of the real people who gather when we preach. A valuable and stimulating resource for beginners and experienced preachers alike."
> —**Linda Lee Clader,** Dean of Academic Affairs and Professor of Homiletics, Church Divinity School of the Pacific and Graduate Theological Union

"Thomas Troeger and H. Edward Everding bring to us a much needed work on preaching to the whole people of God (Bargaining Betty and Conceptualizing Charles and everyone in between). Drawing upon theories of learning they present understandings and strategies for increasing our communication abilities. I try not to miss anything written by Tom Troeger, and pastors will do well not to miss this inclusive approach to our task of preaching."
> —**David Howell,** Editor, Lectionary Homiletics/Good Preacher.com

"Drs. Troeger and Everding demonstrate how to play the homiletical harp for twenty-first-century worshipers. Readers will be well equipped to reach all who gather with the timeless message delivered in relevant ways. This book is a must-read for those preparing for a first appointment and for seasoned sages!"
> —**Safiyah Fosua,** Director, Invitational Preaching Ministries, General Board of Discipleship, The United Methodist Church

"I loved reading this book! It is an outstanding application of cognitive theories to effective preaching, replete with wonderful examples to expand one's repertoire of communicative tools. It's a broadly accessible book that can help us reduce our distortions and stereotypes of those who differ from and with us. Even more significantly, however, it describes and models a hospitable and gracious honoring of the whole person and the whole church. It can open you in new ways to the work of God's Spirit in the church and world while equipping you to be a more effective vessel for that work."
> —**Lucinda Huffaker,** Coauthor, *Viewpoints: Perspectives of Faith and Christian Nurture,* and past Director, Wabash Center for Teaching and Learning in Theology and Religion

CONTENTS

CHAPTER 1

ALL OF US FOR
ALL OF GOD

Preaching That Honors Many Ways of Knowing

ALL OF US

A ll of us for all of God.[1] It sounds simple enough. But try to preach so that the Spirit working through you opens the whole congregation to the glory and wonder of God. You immediately encounter the complexity of who we human creatures are, who God is, and how we interrelate and communicate with one another. Looking out upon the congregation, you are aware that people perceive, process, and respond to your sermons in strikingly different ways.

Sometimes after preaching a sermon I wonder what "all of them" really heard. Listening to their comments, I think: *Is that what I said?* Sometimes I respond "Thank you" because it seems that some of them heard more than I said. I stand amazed how the Spirit can work through my limitations. But other times I regret how my limitations may block the Spirit.

Both of us have learned that the Spirit is not ours to command or control: "The wind/spirit blows where it chooses, and you hear the sound of it, but you do not know where it comes from or where it goes" (John 3:8).[2] No homiletical method can guarantee the Spirit will come to the preacher and the congregation. Yet we believe as Augustine does that "in order to know the truth of what is spoken, I must be taught by him who dwells within and gives me counsel about words spoken externally in the ear."[3] Or as the Protestant reformer John Calvin puts the matter: "For as God alone is a fit witness of himself in his word, so also the word will not find acceptance in men's hearts before it is sealed by the inward testimony of the Spirit."[4] Attending to the Spirit includes relying on the gifts that God gives us, believing that we have received them for a purpose, and trusting that they can strengthen our preaching of the gospel.

The phrase "all of us" points to the multiple ways of knowing that God has bestowed upon us:

Are we possessed with the capacity for deep and passionate feeling? Yes, but we are not limited to feeling.

Do we have the ability to observe, reason, and invent solutions to difficult problems? Yes, but we are not defined by our thought alone.

Are we creatures who can taste the extraordinary variety of the material world? Yes, but our identities are larger than our bodies.

Do our souls flow with visions that keep hope alive and open us to the living God? Yes, but we are not purely spiritual beings.

To engage "all of us for all of God" means, then, to engage the full range of who we are as creatures. Not just our feeling. Not just our thinking. Not just our materiality. Not just our spirituality. But the full, rich treasury of our humanity as created by God, the many varied ways God has given us to perceive, process, and respond to the world. Preachers who engage our multiple capacities for learning and knowing become more effective vessels of the Spirit.

Despite the richness of our resources, most of us have favored ways of learning and knowing, including how we process sermons. Wise pastors know that some of their listeners love stories, while others are listening for what the point is, and still others are waiting to be touched in the depths of their being.

"Draw a picture that will help me see what you are saying."

"Clarify your argument so I can figure out if I agree with you."

"Warm my heart, and I will feel the truth."

The variety of favored ways of knowing suggests that preachers need to draw upon their full humanity in order to communicate effectively with the full humanity of their congregation. By expanding their cognitive repertoire—that is to say, by cultivating the ability to use many ways of learning and knowing in their sermons—preachers can reach a broader range of listeners.

PREACHER-FRIENDLY THEORIES OF LEARNING AND KNOWING

Many preachers intuitively realize that different people learn differently. But we do not have to depend on intuition alone. We can build into sermon preparation the ways of knowing that are evident in people's responses to our sermons. Cognitive learning theory refines our understanding of the act of communication between preacher and congregation. It clarifies how we perceive, process, and respond to the world through many ways of knowing. It helps explain why different congregation members have varied responses to the same sermon. And it adds motivation to be a preacher who "gets up from his or her desk, leaves behind interpretive reading, and goes in search of real bodies to engage in conversation about the text."[5] Listening to the extraordinary range of responses to a biblical text reveals that there are many ways of knowing, and these different ways will play a decisive role in how a sermon is received.

We learn through *feelings* awakened by vocal tone and physical gesture as much as by content. A young boy listening to one preacher who speaks in a harsh voice about God's love turns to his father and asks, "Why is that man so angry?" A couple with tears in their eyes thanks another preacher for sharing a story about embracing grief at the loss of a child.

We learn through *thinking* that sometimes expands the boundaries of conventional thought and sometimes gets interpreted in ways we never intended. One person's comment about our analysis of a difficult biblical text reduces our sermon to a stereotypical idea while another person notes how we challenged her thinking about the passage and opened a new universe of meaning.

We learn through *imagining* that delights some listeners while it distances others. Talking about "the symbol of the resurrection" upsets one group in the congregation while others are grateful because they had never considered interpreting Easter in such a visionary way.

We learn through *doing*, although different people have different ideas of what "doing faith" means. One person comes out grateful for the down-to-earth practical ways we named for applying the sermon to real life, while another found our remarks too simplistic and divorced from reality.

- Feeling
- Thinking
- Imagining
- Doing

Any mode of learning will be interpreted in different ways by different people. But by employing all four modes of learning we increase the communicative range of our preaching because we embrace more completely each individual listener's humanity as well as the variety of learning modes that characterize the congregation as a whole.

Utilizing many ways of knowing, our sermons model how the congregation can do the same. Preachers thereby encourage people to employ God-given abilities that they may have neglected. The person whose passion can be enhanced by precise thought and the person whose logic can be empowered by deeper feeling can learn from the preacher how to achieve a more balanced, holistic faith. It is a faith that fulfills the first commandment to love the Lord our God with all our heart and with all our soul and with all our mind and with all our strength (Mark 12:30).

Our brief review of four modes of learning—feeling, thinking, imagining, doing—introduces the basic pattern of this book. In each chapter we identify a theory about how people perceive, process, and respond to the world so that preachers can become more skilled at using a wide repertoire of communicative means. We will consider three major theories:

- multiple intelligences (often abbreviated MI)
- children's ways of knowing
- adult ways of knowing

In a final chapter we will explore how to bring all three theories together in the act of creating and delivering sermons.

Several times over the last ten years we have team-taught a course in which experienced pastors have crafted sermons using these theories of learning and knowing. Although we would never claim these methods are infallible, we have evidence from the positive response of listeners that sermons employing multiple ways of knowing draw a wider range of people into an encounter with the word of God. We give examples from our students' sermons as well as our own to let you see what the theories look like in practice.

Chapter 2 uses the theory of "multiple intelligences" to explore in detail people's varied ways of learning. Most people gauge "smartness" or intelligence by their linguistic or logical abilities. IQ tests focus primarily on these two cognitive capacities—as do many sermons! It is common to think about a well-crafted sermon in terms of its exquisite use of words and skilled analysis of concepts. Such sermons may be well crafted, but they often fall on deaf ears for many in the congregation. Such sermons fail to engage "all of us." Howard Gardner, who has specialized in studying varied ways of human knowing, has criticized IQ standards because people demonstrate intelligence in many other ways than language and logic alone.[6]

Can you imagine a sermon that takes into account "all of us," when each of us is capable of eight intelligences? This does not mean that every person has developed every intelligence to the highest possible degree. But these intelligences are present among "all of us" in the congregation. Clearly, sermons will employ words and some form of logic. But sermons can also tap into people's abilities to experience their lives through spatial imagery or music or action or interpersonal relations or self-reflection or the natural environment. That might initially seem to be more than you as a preacher can or want to handle. But you will discover that the theory of multiple intelligences provides a usable framework for creating and delivering sermons that engage the actual ways your people compose meaning for their lives.

In chapter 3 we explore children's ways of knowing and in chapter 4 adult ways of knowing. People's varied ways of knowing expand our understanding of how thinking and logic function in sermons. Just as there are different forms of intelligence, so there are different forms of thinking and logic among "all of us." We learn in these chapters how to create and deliver sermons for different ways of knowing. This theory is based on research in cognitive developmental theory.[7]

Through experience and intuition, we sense that "all of us" exemplify different ways of making meaning. We are, for example, aware that children are not miniature adults in their ways of thinking. Children's sermons honor children's ways of knowing, but preaching a children's sermon is not the only way to reach the children. It is possible to preach in a manner that appeals to both adults and children without reducing the sermon to a children's sermon. Although the experienced pastors in our classes were initially skeptical about this, they mastered the method to the delight of their listeners.

As you try out these theories for yourself, we believe you will soon learn, as one of our pastors puts it, "to be mindful of children listening to your sermons and to find ways of bringing them in."

Adults, like children, do not all think the same way. Attention to the variety of adult faith perspectives will provide you with a structure for identifying those different ways of thinking and suggestions about how to use them in sermons.

THOU SHALL NOT LABEL

In all of our explorations we emphasize that it is essential not to label individuals nor to conclude we have their ways of thinking neatly pegged. We begin our course by announcing this commandment in the first class: "Thou shall not label." Rather than place individuals in categories, we encourage preachers to honor children's and adults' varied ways of knowing. We invite preachers to be good neighbors to their congregations, with an understanding of "neighbor" that has been developed by James Nieman and Thomas Rogers: "The neighbor is someone we regularly meet, a fellow participant in social encounters. The word thus designates interaction, not just proximity. At the same time, however, the neighbor is not a member of our household. Scripture may call for a particular treatment of the neighbor . . . but the difference between relatives and neighbors is not thereby erased. . . . [The Good Samaritan] remained, it seems, distinctly Samaritan even in being the quintessential neighbor."[8]

Applying these insights to human cognition and preaching, we realize that people do not all belong to the same "household" of learning and knowing, that our congregations consist of many different neighbors, and that our preaching will not erase their differences. God calls us to make our preaching neighborly to our listeners' varied ways of knowing and thereby to model how they can be neighborly to one another.

We are employing cognitive theories to accomplish the same goal that John McClure approaches through other processes: namely, "to situate preaching as a radical act of compassionate responsibility."[9] Honoring other people's ways of knowing is a way of honoring their humanity, their identity, the unique way in which God has created them. It is "a radical act of compassionate responsibility" because it subverts the oppressive use of language that assumes there is only one way to see and respond to the vast and many-angled complexity of human life.

One experienced pastor who took our course summarized the neighborly spirit that we seek to nurture in preachers: "When preparing a sermon, cognitive theory can guide my creativity by helping me imagine the myriad of ways I can express the same idea. Examining my sermons, teaching style, and content against the perspectives (i.e., modes of thinking) will lead me to be more intentional about the diversity of thought present in a congregation."

PLAYING THE HOMILETICAL HARP FOR A CONGREGATION OF MANY AUDIENCES

Preaching that is "more intentional about the diversity of thought present in a congregation" is more faithful to the apostle Paul's understanding of the church as the Body of Christ, a community gifted in many different ways. Instead of preachers using exclusively their ways of perceiving, processing, and responding, they consider how to engage the variety of gifts that the Spirit gives to the congregation (1 Corinthians 12:4-11). They grow in their ability to preach "what people want to *say* [not hear]. If a minister takes seriously the role of listeners in preaching, there will be sermons expressing for the whole church, and with God as the primary audience, the faith, the doubt, the fear, the anger, the love, the joy, the gratitude that is in all of us. The listeners say, 'Yes, that is my message; that is what I have wanted to say.' All of us recognize here a dynamic that has long been operative in many black churches but which has been absent in traditions in which preachers only speak to but not in and for the faithful community."[10]

To speak "in and for" a community requires understanding not only its idiom but also the many ways that its different members respond to what they see and hear. Concern for preaching the gospel to a congregation of multiple audiences has received extensive attention in recent homiletical literature, yet it is a theme as ancient as the Scriptures. The apostle Paul, though he lived centuries before the advent of developmental psychology, recognized that our forms of thought and expression change as we grow up and mature: "When I was a child, I spoke like a child, I thought like a child, I reasoned like a child; when I became an adult, I put an end to childish ways" (1 Corinthians 13:11).

Paul also adapted how he communicated to the different cultural and religious contexts in which he found himself: "To the Jews I became as a Jew, in order to win Jews. To those under the law I became as one under the law (though I myself am not under the law) so that I might win those under the law...I have become all things to all people, that I might by all means save some. I do it all for the sake of the gospel, so that I may share in its blessings" (1 Corinthians 9:20, 22b-23).

Paul interprets the gospel through the varied ways of knowing that marked the different cultures in which he ministered. He does not change the message to please his hearers. Instead he deals with a very real need that arose in the church as the result of its becoming a community with people from multiple backgrounds and with diverse ways of thinking and expressing themselves. How is a preacher to communicate the gospel to pluralistic communities?

Although "ancient rhetorical arts were not concerned with audience analysis," the church continued to face "the uniquely Christian problem created by the intellectual, social, and economic diversity represented at any given worship service. To this heterogeneity Gregory the Great (ca. 540–604) spoke as no one had before him."[11] Gregory lists thirty-six pairs of opposite kinds of listeners, beginning with

Men and women.
The poor and the rich.
The joyful and the sad.
Prelates and subordinates.
Servants and masters.
The wise of this world and the dull...[12]

For each of the pairings Gregory supplies a brief homily illustrating his principle that "according to the quality of the hearers ought the discourse of teachers to be fashioned, so as to suit all and each for their several needs, and yet never deviate from the art of common edification. For what are the intent minds of hearers but, so to speak, a kind of tight tensions of strings in a harp, which the skillful player, that he may produce a tune not at variance with itself, strikes variously? And for this reason the strings render back a consonant modulation, that they are struck indeed with one quill, but not with one kind of stroke."[13]

To extend Gregory's metaphor, we are using theories of human cognition to help preachers master the varied strokes that are required to sound the homiletical harp in a pluralistic world and church. Many homileticians have been applying themselves to this task as they seek to understand what has come to be called "contextual preaching: Preaching that responds intentionally and dynamically to the social and cultural location within which the preacher prepares and preaches sermons."[14] Much of the work on contextual preaching reflects the interest that theology in general has taken in understanding how culture shapes the practices that mark particular religious communities. Thus, for example, James R. Nieman and Thomas G. Rogers, using the "four cultural frames of *ethnicity, class, displacement* and *beliefs*"[15] explore how the task of "preaching to every pew" involves learning "how to speak beyond one's own cultural home and proclaim the gospel across the boundaries" that divide us.[16]

Nora Tubbs Tisdale reaches across those boundaries by teaching preachers how to fill the anthropological role of a participant observer who attends to the cultures and subcultures that make up a particular congregation. Her reflections on how a sermon that brings the gospel alive in one congregation may fail in another are very much in harmony with our experience. Because different cultures nurture different ways of knowing, our use of learning theory expands a preacher's range of tools for the cultural analysis of congregations.[17]

Howard Gardner, the scholar who developed MI theory, understands the inescapable impact of culture upon human knowing. Although he considers the brain "the ultimate arbiter among competing accounts of cognition,"[18] Gardner acknowledges that "we cannot (even should we wish to) neatly factor culture out of this [neurobiological] equation, because culture influences every individual (except possibly some freaks) and will, therefore, necessarily color the way that intellectual potentials evolve from the first."[19]

In summary, the phrase "all of us" embraces all that God made us to be: our neurobiological creaturehood, our culturally shaped practices and idioms, our multiple ways of learning and knowing, and the astounding variation in all these aspects of our humanity that is manifest in our communities and congregations. It is a level of complexity that can boggle a preacher's mind. But the theories of MI, children's ways of knowing, and adult ways of knowing are three highly useful tools for understanding the complexity. They help us create and deliver sermons to the whole person and the whole congregation, sermons that engage all of us for all of God.

ALL OF GOD

The phrase "all of God" carries a richness every bit as great or even greater than the phrase "all of us." Just think of the number of names and images for God that are in the Bible alone. Then add to that their subsequent development through hymnody, corporate prayer, the visual arts, poetry, music, and myriads of liturgical practices developed in various cultures and eras of history. This extravagant abundance of images and names for the divine is a warning and an invitation. It is a warning to preachers not to reduce God to some humanly manageable size, a deity small enough to fit the limits of our thought and feeling and the constraints of our faith and practice.

The abundance of names and images for God is also an invitation, an invitation to expand our love and knowledge of the One in whom "we live and move and have our being" (Acts 17:28). The phrase "all of God" beckons us to use every gift that God has given us as a way of knowing God more profoundly. Since God is the source of "every perfect gift" (James 1:17)—including the gift of multiple ways of knowing—it follows that the more we know about those ways, the more we know about the One who created us with these gifts. The knowledge of God and the knowledge of ourselves are mutually illuminating: the more we know God, the more we know ourselves, and the more we know ourselves, the more we know God.

A More Gracious Vision of One Another

Our greater awareness of different ways of knowing affects not only our relationship to God but also our relationship to one another. We become attuned to the richness in others, their particular ways of perceiving, processing, and responding to the world. We gain a more expansive vision, one that is gracious to those who see the world in a different light from ourselves. We begin to live more faithfully not only the first commandment, but also the second commandment: to love our neighbors as ourselves.

To appreciate the grace of such behavior, think of a time when, no matter how hard you tried, you were not able to get your point of view heard, perhaps in a conversation or on the job or in a seminar or at a board meeting. You spoke but you obviously did not get through. Your perspective was either ignored or dismissed out of hand. Then someone had the kindness to stop the conversation and to ask you questions, to listen to your answers, and to try out tentative interpretations of what you were saying, all the while checking with you to see if he or she was hearing you rightly. He or she made an obvious effort to enter your world, to use your idiom, to practice your way of perceiving and responding to things. If you have ever had this happen, then you know how the heart can fill with gratitude when someone else honors another person's way of holding the world together in one's head.

The experience of one human being working hard to understand another is an analogy about what happens when we give all of us to all of God, when we try to understand the word of God and the world of the congregation using many ways of knowing. We honor their perspectives in the same way that the conscientious listener honored our perspective. We will never become God or the congregation, and we will never see life precisely as God or the congregation sees it. Instead, we will come to that blessed point of wisdom where "all our attempts to control, manipulate or understand the other as an object within our world begin to give way to an openness to the other as truly *other*."[20] Without the illusion of mastering them, we will become more attuned to the multiple dimensions of God's word and the varied ways a congregation receives that word. Both God and the congregation will feel toward us some of the same gratitude that filled our hearts when someone honored our ways of perceiving and understanding.

Preaching in a manner that honors the congregation's ways of knowing is not the same as telling them what they want to hear. There is research that reveals people do not want preachers to pander to them. "The collective wisdom of listeners interviewed in the Listening to Listeners Project is also clear on this. Many of them tell us that they rely on the preacher to bring a word from God that may not match their own interests or desires."[21] In fact, congregation members are glad for sermons that challenge and expand their world. However, preachers cannot expand a world they themselves have never entered. When preachers use ways of perceiving, processing, and responding that characterize their listeners' lives, then their sermons awaken affection and trust. Communication improves because the empathic quality of the relationship improves. This insight is preserved in the idiom of common speech when we say, "Now you're talking my language." Such preaching takes the listeners seriously by honoring the unique way God has created them as learning, knowing, thinking, feeling, dreaming creatures.

Preaching that engages people's multiple capacities for understanding and expressing themselves is also much less apt to become manipulative than when we engage only a narrow range of their intelligence. Think of tyrants. Think of advertisers trying to sell you what you do not need. Think of people hell-bent on getting their way no matter how destructive it may be to others. Think of preachers bound to coerce their listeners into believing what they consider to be the only valid response to the gospel of Christ. When people want to manipulate others, they do not appeal to the whole humanity of persons. Instead, they single out one particular human capacity. They use reason alone to design a lockstep argument that stage by stage leads to one inevitable conclusion. Or they engage our feelings at a highly vulnerable point. Or they offer a vision that may be unrealistic but is so soothing to our bruised souls that we abandon our soundest thought and our wisest intuitions. We are not embraced by the grace of God but trapped by the preacher's manipulation.

By way of contrast, the first commandment is utterly nonmanipulative because it requires that our relationship to God involve the sum total of all our ways of being and acting, learning and knowing. Any one sermon may need to draw more upon one human capacity than others: there are times of crisis when a preacher must rigorously appeal to reason. There are times of joy or sadness that call for the release of heartfelt emotion. But over the long haul a preacher needs to nurture the wholeness of the relationship to God that is called for by the great commandment, and this goal requires that the majority of our sermons will employ multiple ways of learning and knowing.

A HOMILETICAL SPIRITUALITY OF WHOLENESS

As the news of Christ spread around the Mediterranean basin in the centuries following the writing of the Gospels and the Epistles, the church, particularly through the writings of St. Augustine, adapted classical rhetoric to the task of preaching. Ancient rhetoric supplied rules and principles for creating and delivering a persuasive public speech. Because it focused on the occasion—legal or ceremonial or political—when the orator would speak, rhetoric emphasized the issue of persuasion while giving less attention to the active role of the listeners. We have already cited Richard Lischer's observation that "the ancient rhetorical arts were not concerned with audience analysis." However, there is a way in which our concern with honoring a congregation's multiple intelligences of learning and knowing reinforces the goals of classical rhetoric "to prove (*probare*), to delight (*delectate*) and to stir or move (*flectere*)."[22]

Lucy Hogan, a homiletician trained in classical rhetoric, cites the three proofs that Aristotle considered essential to persuasive public

speech: *ethos*, the trustworthy character of the speaker; *pathos*, the desire
and ability "to move a group of people to action"; and *logos*, "the actual
words and arguments constructed for the speech."[23] She observes that
when the three dimensions of classical rhetoric "are in balance, the
speaker has a much better chance of convincing his or her listeners."[24]
Hogan's statement resonates with the holistic communication that we are
advocating, and it suggests how we can overcome the suspicion of rhetoric that has haunted homiletics for centuries. Hogan summarizes this historic conflict: "There was a significant tension in the early church
between the Jewish understanding of inspiration and the classical
approach to rhetoric, or the training of speakers. Is the preacher one who
can be taught and trained? Is the preacher the mouthpiece of God who is
entirely dependent upon inspiration? If we look at the life of Augustine,
we see both this tension and the compromise that has lasted over fifteen
hundred years."[25]

Fifteen hundred years is long enough for the compromise between
rhetoric and inspiration! It is time to move to a more faithful, more
sophisticated, less polarized, less simplistic understanding of the interre-
lationship of human preparation and divine inspiration. Faithful preaching that honors the varied ways human beings learn fills the rhetorical
ideal of proving, delighting, and moving. No one faculty of cognition is
granted the highest place of honor. Thought disciplines feeling without
displacing it. Feeling expands the reach of thought. Imagination lifts
visions of what we could do by the grace of God. The realties of human
limitation correct the extravagance of what we imagine. All that God
made us to be works in concert with the Creator. Our preaching becomes
a persuasive witness to the gospel because it appeals to the listeners' multiple capacities for learning and knowing.

When we employ a wide cognitive repertoire in our sermons, we move
beyond the historic compromise between rhetoric and inspiration.
Instead of the two being in tension with each other, our rhetoric—
informed by cognitive theories—becomes a way of preparing ourselves for
inspiration. We begin to embody in our sermons the very way of being
and living to which God calls us. Rhetoric and inspiration are not a

polarity but a continuum. Homiletics thus becomes more than a method of public proclamation. Homiletics is a form of spirituality that opens both preacher and congregation to the living presence of God by employing multiple ways of learning and knowing.

Preaching to the Whole Person in an Age of Religious Violence and Spiritual Hunger

There are people who will be terrified by the phrase "all of us for all of God." If they see you reading this book, they may shudder to think what terror you are concocting in your heart. Since religious faith has often fueled prejudice, holy wars, and oppression, and since these distortions continue to plague the human community, some people will conclude that the last thing we need is a book about preaching that aims to engage all of us for all of God. It sounds like a recipe to feed a crusader's blind mission against whoever is perceived to be the enemy. Is not giving all we are to all of God the root of religious fanaticism?

During the time we were writing this book, a full-scale intellectual debate about this very matter was being waged in many newspapers, magazines, and book reviews as well as on line and on television. We do not have room here to document all of these venues, but we will briefly trace one representative exchange, because the debate about whether religious faith is a force for good or for evil shows no signs of abating. It is part of the context in which we are urging preachers to engage all of us for all of God. We want to be clear that what we are promoting will lessen, not exacerbate, the distorted uses of religious faith.

On March 12, 2006, Slavoj Zizek published an essay in the *New York Times* entitled "Defenders of the Faith." Zizek attempts to make a case for abandoning religion and embracing atheism. Although we have a deep and abiding belief in God, we can follow the line of reasoning that has driven Zizek to his position. He writes: "The lesson of today's terrorism is that if God exists, then everything, including blowing up thousands of innocent bystanders, is permitted—at least to those who claim to act directly on behalf of God, since, clearly, a direct link to God justifies the violation of any merely human constraints and considerations."

Seeking an alternative to religious belief and the violence that it has engendered, Zizek asks a challenging question: "Two years ago, Europeans were debating whether the preamble of the European Constitution should mention Christianity as a key component of the European legacy.... But where [in this discussion] was modern Europe's most precious legacy, that of atheism?"

Given that we live in an age of religious violence, Zizek's rejection of religion is understandable, even though we ourselves are religious people and do not share his conviction. The letters in response to Zizek[26] reveal that there are more nuanced voices hungering to be heard amidst the current theological cacophony. Reading these letters suggests that there are indeed people ready to respond to the more holistic homiletic that we are proposing.

One reader points out that "by comparing only atheists and fundamentalists, Mr. Zizek leaves out the large group of believers who do not support the radical ideas of fundamentalist movements." The writer goes on to identify himself as "one of those moderate believers" whose integrity and moral values are more complex than Zizek understood.

Another respondent also picks up on the oversimplification of the issue, and writes: "Like Islam and Christianity, atheism is characterized by belief. There is nothing inherent to atheism that encourages more or less tolerance than any other religion does."

Finally, an ordained minister writes: "Mr. Zizek is surely right that atheists can be highly moral people, and that religion can bear evil as well as good fruit. But his notion that atheism is 'perhaps our only chance for peace' is as naïve as the outmoded idea that the religious are necessarily better people than atheists.... The path to peace lies in the cooperation of all who are willing to resist such fanaticism—believers and atheists alike."

Imagine if we had written to the paper a letter carrying the byline "All of Us for All of God." Given the volatility of the debate, that might have created a flood of rejoinders asking: Is not giving all of us to all of God the root cause of religious fanaticism?

No, not at all. The distortion of religious faith stems from giving only some of who we are to a truncated vision of God. The violence and brutality of religion arise because of a failure to engage the fullness of our humanity with the fullness of God. Feeling runs untested by reason's light. Thought becomes entirely calculating without any heartfelt compassion. The visionary imagination throws ethical considerations to the wind. We give ourselves up to the ecstasy of being part of an unthinking mob. When any of these things happen, then we have not given all of us to all of God. We have done the opposite. We have abandoned the major portion of what God has made us to be. We have heated a fragmentary piece of our humanity to a feverish intensity, and dedicated it to an idol that we have fashioned from an image of one isolated aspect of God.

When we give all of us to all of God, then faith becomes a process of allowing our various ways of knowing to correct and balance one another in light of the fullness of the divine—a fullness that awakens humility, not arrogance—as we come to realize how impartial and imperfect all our knowledge is. We are excited about theories of learning and knowing because they can help preachers communicate the gospel more effectively. But an even greater impetus for our work is to provide an approach to preaching that nurtures the restorative and healing functions of religious faith rather than its distortions.

The antidote to the rotten theology of destructive religious faith is not the abandonment of theology, but sound theology. Theories of learning and knowing can help preachers root their sermons in core theological values that make religion a positive force for good. When we engage all of us for all of God we embody:

• a *theological anthropology* that takes seriously all that God has made us to be, all of our multiple capacities for perceiving, processing, and responding

• an *ecclesiology* that honors the varied gifts in the Body of Christ

• a *doctrine of the fullness of God* celebrating that God is both revealed and hidden, that there is always room for us to grow in the knowledge and love of the divine

• a *commitment to live the two greatest commandments* as a way of promoting a balanced, vital, faithful relationship to God and our neighbors.

Augustine believed that the ultimate test for the interpretation of Scripture is the degree to which it helps people fulfill the two greatest commandments: "So if it seems to you that you have understood the divine scriptures, or any part of them, in such a way that by this understanding you do not build up this twin love of God and neighbor, then you have not yet understood them."[27] Augustine is so convinced of his principle that he believes if people are mistaken in an interpretation of scripture but their intent is "to build up charity, which is *the end of the law* (1 Tm 1:5), they are mistaken in the same sort of way as people who go astray off the road, but still proceed by rough paths to the same place as the road was taking them."[28] Augustine goes on to affirm the importance of interpreting the Scriptures accurately—he is not eager to encourage or excuse shoddy biblical interpretation!

We aim to encourage the graciousness that arises from Augustine's affirmation of the two greatest commandments. Drawing upon our multiple cognitive capacities will help us interpret Scripture in a way that is theologically richer and more faithful to the living presence of God and the needs of our neighbors. As Paul Wilson puts the issue: "Instead of being conceived primarily as a rule book or answer book, in this understanding the biblical text is conceived primarily as a book of invitation to a life of risk on behalf of the neighbor and faith in a God who abundantly and graciously provides for all needs."[29]

In future chapters we will see that the images of the Bible "as a rule book or answer book" arise from particular ways of knowing. Is there truth to these images of the Bible? Yes. There are rules in the Bible without which life falls apart. For example, the Ten Commandments. There are also answers in the Bible to some of life's most central questions: Does God love me? What does God require of us? Rules and answers have a place in biblical interpretation and in the life of faith. But at the same time learning theory makes us intensely aware that if the Bible is "conceived *primarily* as a rule book or answer book," then we distort the Scriptures by neglecting many other perspectives and modes of cognition that are found within the Bible and among its readers.

Because the goal of our work is to help preachers nurture a healthy, holistic relationship to God, we find our homiletic naturally begins with prayer—prayer that is as honest and candid as the psalmist's in sharing both our resistance and our desire to give all that we are to all that God is:

If all you want, Lord, is my heart,
my heart is yours alone,
providing I may set apart
my mind to be my own.

If all you want, Lord, is my mind,
my mind belongs to you,
but let my heart remain inclined
to do what it would do.

If heart and mind would both suffice,
while I kept strength and soul,
at least I would not sacrifice
completely my control.

But since, O God, you want them all
to shape with your own hand,
I pray for grace to heed your call
to live your first command.[30]

CHAPTER 2

MULTIPLE INTELLIGENCES

Preachers and Congregations Are Smarter Than We Think

THE PREACHER ARTIST, THE PREACHER COACH

We begin with two stories about preachers that we will then interpret by introducing the theory of multiple intelligences (MI).

I (Tom) once had a student in an introductory preaching course who was a professional visual artist. She had been highly successful, doing graphics and design work for clients around the world. An active lay-woman in church, she started theological school in her middle years while continuing to work as an artist. I had seen some of her work, and I understood why she had been so successful. Whether it was a realistic drawing or an abstraction or a logo designed for a business, every line and color worked in concert to produce something that delighted the eye.

But when she preached her first sermon in class, not one of us could follow her train of thought. She spoke clearly enough. Most of her individual sentences made sense, and a few even hinted at deeper meanings worth exploring. But by the time she finished, we were all wondering what the sermon as a whole meant. The artist was a gracious woman, and she appreciated the class's honest assessment that her first effort at preaching was incoherent to them.

I worked with her on developing a sermonic structure that listeners could follow, but we made little progress. Finally, I asked her if she would go home and draw a picture of what was taking place in the biblical story on which her sermon was based. She returned with a powerful drawing. A publisher would have been glad to use it for a book cover or a museum to claim it for its collection. I then asked her to describe exactly what was happening in the drawing and why she pictured things the way she did. Words started flowing from her. Even without the picture in front of my eyes, I could follow everything she was saying. Then and there in my office she preached a comprehensible and meaningful sermon, rough here and there, but still easy to follow and with substantial theological depth.

In another homiletics class I had a student who had been a high school gym teacher and a coach for the football, basketball, and baseball teams. When he walked across the chancel and stood in the pulpit, you might have guessed his background. He was in good shape. His posture and gestures had the grace of a fine athlete. He was also an excellent storyteller. Every sermon was filled with stories from his years of coaching, some hilarious, some serious and sad. He had the good homiletical sense not to use the stories merely to entertain us. He artfully related them to the Scriptures and to our lives. Nevertheless, after listening to him several times, the class, as much as they liked his stories, acknowledged that they hungered for material from other areas of life than only athletics. Some of them, particularly those who identified themselves as "not athletic" or "not interested in sports," wondered if he could bring in music or literature or movies or television or news.

THINKING INVOLVES THINKING MORE THAN ONE WAY

The stories of the preacher artist and the preacher coach demonstrate that thinking involves thinking in more than one way. As long as I worked with the artist only by thinking in words, she was not able to achieve the verbal clarity she needed as a preacher. But when she engaged her capacity for visual thinking, her sermons became vivid and much easier to follow. Her favored way of thinking was through her keen eye and its relationship to the finesse of her arm and hand with a pencil, a brush, a crayon, a pallet. By beginning with her favored way of thinking, the artist preacher was able to strengthen her less developed way of thinking.

The coach was coherent from his first sermon, easy to follow and delighting his listeners. He used his ability to think about the athletic use of the body and team sports as a way of holding his sermons together. Using his favored way of thinking, he preached well from the start. But over time, his bodily thinking failed to feed the hunger of the congregation because their favored ways of thinking were inadequately engaged.

Placed side by side, the stories of the artist preacher and the coach preacher reveal both the strength and the weakness of preaching from our favored ways of thinking. The strength is that it involves using our most developed capacities for perceiving and responding to the world. We create sermons that are vivid, and our delivery comes across as authentic.[1] The artist became a coherent preacher when she worked from her artistic strength. The coach was immediately rational and clear because he worked from his extensive experience in athletics. They were at their best when they preached from what they knew best.

But there is a weakness in preaching from *only* our favored ways of thinking: we do not communicate as fully as we would like to with congregation members whose favored ways of thinking are different from our own. The preacher artist could not always be preaching a visually organized sermon, and the preacher coach could not always be preaching from his athletic experience. Both needed to expand their cognitive repertoires in order to engage their congregations more effectively. For a sermon is not simply what the preacher says, it is also what the congregation hears, and that depends on how the listeners perceive, process, and respond to what is preached.

Reuel Howe describes the congregation members as our "partners in preaching."[2] We like that word *partner*. It suggests to us the image of a dance. When you dance you have to coordinate your movements with those of your partner. When you preach you have to coordinate your favored ways of thinking with the congregation's.

Howe developed a sophisticated understanding of the partnership between preacher and congregation. He realized that every time a preacher delivers a sermon there are effectively three different sermons: (1) the preacher's sermon, (2) each individual listener's sermon, and (3) the cumulative effect of sermons 1 and 2 upon the congregation as a corporate body: "The minister preaches his [or her] sermon in order that other sermons may be brought into being in the congregation, sermons that will be the joint products of both his [or her] and the congregation's effort."[3] Howe names the third sermon "the church's sermon, the joint product of the preacher's message and the congregation's meanings expressed through their listening.... We call it the 'church's sermon' because it *is* the joint creation of the preacher and members of the congregation."[4]

Howe realized there are many barriers that can hinder the creation of the church's sermon. He names them "meaning barriers." They include language, images, differences, anxieties, and defensiveness. These barriers can work in preacher and congregation alike. They often result from the associations that we have with certain words and symbols: "The word 'Bible,' for example, can have a repressive moralistic meaning for one person because the Bible and its teaching was used to suppress gay and spontaneous responses during his childhood. Another person will have joyous and constructive meanings for the Bible because it was used to elicit responses of trust and love."[5] Since these associations and the memories they evoke are a function of something larger than language alone, Howe concludes that meaningful communication "is not only a matter of semantics."[6] It requires far more than clarifying the dictionary meaning of words and the arrangement of phrases and sentences in grammatically comprehensible sentences: "In the actual preaching encounter much, then, will depend on how well both preacher and people have used their eyes and ears prior to the encounter.... [The preacher] must learn to see as well as to hear what his [or her] people are communicating and what the world in which they both live is communicating."[7]

We find Howe's analysis to be so perceptive that we introduce it during the first class meeting of our course on preaching and theories of knowing. It helps everyone to be clear whose sermon they are talking about. Are they talking about the preacher's sermon? By preacher's sermon we mean the sum total of everything the preacher says and does: the content, the vocal inflection, the gestures, the posture, the pace, the pauses, the facial expressions, where the eyes focus, and the multiple intelligences that are used. Everything. Or are they talking about sermon number two: the sermon touched off in them as individuals, including the memories, feelings, and multiple intelligences that were engaged in them? Or are they talking about the church's sermon: the sense of its meaning for them as a gathered community who through the coming week will scatter into many different worlds? Without such clarity, we may talk about the sermon touched off in ourselves and assume it is the same for everyone, for the preacher and the rest of the class or congregation. But while we are talking, the preacher is thinking, "That is not the sermon I delivered," and other listeners are thinking, "That is not the sermon I heard."[8]

The theory of multiple intelligences (MI) expands our understanding of what Howe called barriers to communication, barriers to "the sermons that will be the joint products of both [the preacher's] and the congregation's effort." MI theory supports Howe's insight that much more than semantics is involved in good communication, and it gives us tools for analyzing why a sermon was or was not an effective act of communication for particular people. But even more than this, MI theory supplies us with tools for amplifying the repertoire of the ways of knowing that we employ in our preaching.

USING MI TO OVERCOME BARRIERS BETWEEN PREACHER AND CONGREGATION

Any form of human communication presupposes understandings of intelligence. If I say to somebody, "Don't you get it?" my question implies that my words should easily be understood by anyone who really listened to what I said. My frustrated vocal tone implies that my uncomprehending listener is not very smart. For the most part, in Western culture intelligence is defined in terms of language and logic. IQ testing presupposes this model. But that model does not begin to exhaust the human potential for being smart.[9] If language and logic alone constituted what it means to be intelligent, then preaching to "all of us" would require that we focus exclusively on those two capacities of the human mind. But we know by intuition that logic and language do not begin to account for vast domains of our knowledge and experience. Consider this famous sonnet by Elizabeth Barrett Browning. Her language points to ways of knowing that extend far beyond the circumference of her words:

> How do I love thee? Let me count the ways.
> I love thee to the depth and breadth and height
> My soul can reach, when feeling out of sight
> For the ends of Being and ideal Grace.
> I love thee to the level of every day's
> Most quiet need, by sun and candle-light.
> I love thee freely, as men strive for right;
> I love thee purely, as they turn from praise,
> I love thee with the passion put to use
> In my old griefs, and with my childhood's faith.
> I love thee with a love I seemed to lose
> With my lost saints—I love thee with the breath,
> Smiles, tears of all my life!—and, if God choose,
> I shall but love thee better after death.[10]

To love someone with "the breath,/Smiles, tears of all my life" is a form of knowing that goes beyond language and logic. How impoverished our lives would be without such knowledge! To have this knowledge is to be wise in the ways of love. It is a wisdom that logic alone will never command.

We have used the example of Barrett's love poem, but her appeal to ways of knowing that extend beyond language and logic can be replicated in many other areas of human experience. Howard Gardner helps us understand analytically the expanded range of intelligence that the poet employs intuitively.[11] Preachers can gain from Gardner's work increased competence to create sermons that engage the whole person and the whole congregation.

Gardner defines an intelligence "as a bio-psychological potential to process information that can be activated in a cultural setting to solve problems or create products that are of value in a culture."[12] To identify a distinct intelligence, Gardner developed eight criteria drawn from biological sciences, logical analysis, developmental psychology, and traditional psychological research. These resources led him to understand the human brain or mind "as a series of relatively separate faculties, with only loose and non-predictable relations with one another, than as a single, all-purpose machine that performs steadily at a certain horsepower, independent of content and context."[13]

As we write this book, Gardner has identified eight separate intelligences. When we first started teaching together about his theory, Gardner had identified only seven that met his rigorous definition of a distinctive intelligence. He considered the possibilities of spiritual and moral intelligences (he labels these as existential intelligence), but could not justify them according to the criteria he used in determining the validity of any of the other intelligences.[14] However, the eight intelligences that he has identified can help preachers speak more effectively about spiritual and moral concerns because such matters involve people's many ways of knowing.

The increase from seven to eight intelligences reveals that MI is a dynamic theory that may develop in ways not yet foreseen. Nevertheless, we have found Gardner's present itemization of eight intelligences remarkably helpful to preachers seeking to bring the gospel to the whole person and the whole congregation.

EIGHT INTELLIGENCES: EIGHT WAYS OF ENGAGING ALL OF US FOR ALL OF GOD

Here is an outline of how we will introduce you to the eight intelligences and their implications for engaging all of us for all of God:

- First we list them and give you Gardner's own definition of their distinctive character.
- Then we look at the implications of each one of them for preaching.
- We follow this with an exercise to help teach MI theory to a congregation as a way of honoring their many different gifts.
- Next we provide a chart to help you remember more easily the eight intelligences.
- Finally, we lead you through a sample Bible study that uses all eight intelligences in the preparation of a sermon.

Gardner defines the eight intelligences. (The numbering is for convenience. It does not imply favoring one over the other.)

1. "*Linguistic intelligence* involves sensitivity to spoken and written language, the ability to learn languages, and the capacity to use language to accomplish certain goals."[15]

2. "*Logical-mathematical intelligence* involves the capacity to analyze problems logically, carry out mathematical operations, and investigate issues scientifically."[16]

3. "*Musical intelligence* entails skill in performance, composition, and appreciation of musical patterns."[17]

4. "*Bodily-kinesthetic intelligence* entails the potential of using one's whole body or parts of the body (like the hand or the mouth) to solve problems or fashion products."[18]

5. "*Spatial intelligence* features the potential to recognize and manipulate the patterns of wide space (those used, for instance, by navigators and pilots) as well as patterns of more confined areas (such as those of importance to sculptors, surgeons, chess players, graphic artists, or architects)."[19]

6. "*Interpersonal intelligence* denotes a person's capacity to understand the intentions, motivations, and desires of other people and, consequently, to work effectively with others."[20]

7. "*Intrapersonal intelligence* involves the capacity to understand oneself, to have an effective working model of oneself—including one's own

desires, fears, and capacities—and to use such information effectively in regulating one's life."[21]

8. *Naturalist intelligence* involves "expertise in the recognition and classification of the numerous species—the flora and fauna—of his or her environment."[22]

Let us now consider what each intelligence implies for preaching the word of God to the whole person and the whole congregation. Gardner's definitions ascribe two or three distinctive characteristics to each intelligence. We can use these different characteristics to assess more precisely the particular ways in which we engage any single intelligence. Our exploration will help us map both the intelligences our preaching favors, and the characteristics that dominate our way of communicating.

The *linguistic intelligence* is one that most preachers have generally developed to a high degree of proficiency. It has three definitive characteristics:

- sensitivity to spoken and written language,
- the ability to learn languages,
- and the capacity to use language to accomplish certain goals.

Gardner's specificity about *both* spoken and written language is significant. Because of the nature of academic theological study and the education that precedes it, many students learn how to write essays, but may have had little or no instruction in the art of oral public communication. Good academic students often stand to preach for the first time and their sermon sounds like a read essay instead of the proclamation of the gospel. They need to engage more fully the spoken dimension of their linguistic intelligence. Fortunately, there are a number of homiletical works that suggest very practical ways of strengthening the arts of oral communication.[23]

One way we encourage more affective speaking in our courses is to require that students use what we call oral/aural writing.[24] Our syllabus includes instructions to write:

Like this.
Not the long sentences of written prose.
But brief sentences.
Words and clauses.
Each one getting a line.

This is the way we talk.
The way we listen.
How we hear.
Develop your ear for speech.
How words are heard.
Or lip read.
Now and then you can get away with a longer sentence such as the one
you are reading at this moment.
But.
That's for the eye.
Not the ear.
It makes for hard listening.

And it makes for getting lost while preaching!
Tangled language
becomes tangled revelation,
an obstacle course
for the congregation,
for the heart hungering for God.
Short lines
are easier to follow.
Especially,
if you're nervous.

Play around with this method.
Play with language.
Play with different ways of thinking.
Of seeing.

Of being.
Of communicating.

Kind of fun—
isn't it?
It will open you to the Spirit.
And your congregation too.

The second aspect of Gardner's linguistic intelligence is "the ability to learn languages." We all learned our native language as children, and many of us later learn a second or third language. Some preachers learn biblical Hebrew and Greek, and all effective preachers learn "the language" of their congregations. They become fluent in the local idiom and the dominant ways that their communities articulate their experience and worldview.[25]

Gardner's third characteristic of linguistic intelligence is the "capacity to use language to accomplish certain goals." The forms of ancient rhetoric that have influenced centuries of Christian preaching took persuasion as their goal.[26] The purpose of a speech or a sermon was to "persuade" the listeners of a particular truth. Recent homiletical theory has expanded the meaning of the word *rhetoric* to embrace the wide range of ways that a preacher may use symbols, images, stories, and other devices for conveying and composing meaning in a congregation. Instead of focusing on persuasion, this broader view of rhetoric encourages preachers to identify with their listeners so that their sermons connect with the congregation's life and faith. Such identification "involves more than empathy. It involves the ability to actually take on another person's entire mode of being and communicating, at nearly every possible level."[27] The theory of MI helps us realize this goal of identification while maintaining "respect for the listener as truly *other*"[28] by honoring the different ways they perceive and process the world and by not insisting that they hold things together in their heads in the same way that we do.

The *logical-mathematical intelligence* involves three definitive character-istics:
- the capacity to analyze problems logically,
- carry out mathematical operations,
- and investigate issues scientifically.

Although theological education values the teaching of critical think-ing, it usually does not feature courses in calculus and the physical sci-ences. However, the logical-mathematical intelligence can make a sermon come alive in any number of ways. Consider, for example, how logical analysis and mathematics enliven the interpretation of the fol-lowing biblical verse: "Mary took a pound of costly perfume made of pure nard, anointed Jesus' feet, and wiped them with her hair. The house was filled with the fragrance of the perfume" (John 12:3).

A pound of perfume.
One whole pound!
Do you ever visit the perfume counter in a store?
Perhaps you are going to buy
a fragrance for yourself
or for someone you love.
On the counter you find several tiny crystal bottles,
each topped with an atomizer.
You squeeze the rubber ball at one end
aiming the nozzle at the back of your wrist.
An infinitesimal spray lands on your skin.
[The preacher takes a long inhalation
while holding up one wrist to the nose.]
If it's good perfume,
that is all you need.
It does not take much.
Let's assume that the entire bottle
contains one ounce.
And that one ounce

is good for a thousand sample sprays.
A clerk stands by the counter
making sure people don't take more
than a single spray.
This stuff costs!
One spray,
and the scent stays with you all day.

Now the biblical text says
Mary poured a pound of costly perfume
on Jesus' feet.
She did not spray it with an atomizer.
She poured it.
It was not a sample
of infinitesimal droplets.
It was liquid.
A pound of liquid.
A pound is 16 ounces.
That would be 16,000 times as much perfume
as a single spray to the back of your wrist.
16,000 times as much!
[The preacher takes one great long, loud, sustained inhalation.]
No wonder
"The house was filled with the fragrance of the perfume."
Not just the dining room.
Not just the kitchen.
Not just the sleeping areas.
But the whole house.
And if they opened the doors and the windows,
passers in the street would smell it:
Mary's extravagance wafting out into the world.
I wonder what would happen
if we were that extravagant
with our gratitude toward Christ.

Notice here how the analytical reasoning and the math give a weight to the final sentence that it would not carry without the numerical calculations. Far from making the sermon dry, they make it more vivid. They help us draw out a detail from the text—"a pound of costly perfume"—and develop its theological significance. It may surprise us preachers how often our logical-mathematical intelligence can enhance biblical exposition, especially when the text makes some precise observation that invites us to "go do the math," or when scientific exactitude puts common human proclivities in a new light. Here for example is an experienced preacher from one of our courses using the logical-mathematical intelligence to help his congregation reframe their impatience with community prayer that takes longer than they expected:

Oh, we know God is worth 5 or 6 extra minutes—
God: the Maker of heaven and earth;
Creator of comets and planets and stars and galaxies;
God, whose hand somehow shaped the human genome
into a precise DNA sequence of 3 billion proteins
that makes each of us a living, breathing, thinking miracle!
But when the minute hand creeps past the noon hour,
we start getting a little grouchy, don't we?[29]

The logical-mathematical intelligence can do more for preaching than enrich biblical exposition and pastoral guidance. Its third characteristic, the ability to "investigate issues scientifically," is essential when preachers want to provide prophetic wisdom on such topics as medical ethics, world hunger, the AIDS crisis, and environmental devastation. We have discovered that there are many scientists and scientifically minded listeners who hunger for the mutual illumination of faith and science. We think here of a scientist who, grateful for my words that related faith and science, took time to e-mail me (Tom). First, he identified himself: "I am not a politician or a preacher—instead, I am a scientist." Then he went on to affirm in his own words the spirit of what I had expressed, that "science can be a form of worship of God the creator." It was a small exchange but a significant one. It shows what can happen when we engage people's dominant ways of knowing.

The *musical intelligence* entails
- skill in performance,
- composition,
- and appreciation of musical patterns.

In American culture the musical intelligence is both prized and abused. Just think of the number of people who walk around insulated from the sounds of their immediate environment because they are listening to their tunes on an iPod or Walkman. It is clear that the third characteristic, appreciation of musical patterns, is commonly celebrated in one way or another by nearly all of us.

But if we look at the first two characteristics, skill in performance and composition, then we find a culture that depends more on professional music-making than our own talent. One of our colleagues, Patrick Evans, a professional singer and cantor for our daily chapel services at Yale Divinity School, has pointed out that ours is one of the few societies in which there are people who claim they cannot carry a tune. In most cultures everyone sings or plays an instrument. Making music is integral to their work and play, their celebrations and rituals. But in American society, although music is ubiquitous, it is generally provided by others. The result is the atrophy of the musical intelligence in large numbers of the population, who come to the faulty conclusion that they have no musical intelligence. This is reinforced by mean remarks to children—"Move your lips but do not make a sound"—and a television show, *American Idol*, that makes fun of people's efforts to sing. Different factors work together to suppress the musical intelligence in many people. Being told early on in our lives that we cannot do something may haunt us through every stage of development. John Bell tells of a group of adults that shared the voices from their childhood echoing down through their lives: "It became transparent that no matter how sophisticated, cultured, articulate or capable people are in their adult lives, the voices they heard in their childhood can still disable them.

"It is exactly the same for those who believe they cannot sing because someone once told them so. Across the years the pronouncement of doom reverberates."[30]

Yet most preachers know the astounding value of music, how it gives wings to words and often is a vessel of the Spirit. We have heard many excellent preachers who in the midst of a sermon or at its conclusion have broken into singing, and the song lifted us toward the realities they had proclaimed. Whenever I (Tom) play my flute in the course of a sermon, there are several listeners who say, "I really got what you were saying when the music started." I cannot speak and play my instrument simultaneously! So what happens in such cases is that engaging the musical intelligence facilitates the engagement of the linguistic intelligence.

We believe the church has long known intuitively about the musical intelligence, and that is one reason worship services in nearly all traditions interweave word and music. "The proper relationship of the sound of worship to the voice of the sermon is what I want to call the acoustemology of the church. Epistemology is philosophical reflection on how we know what we know. Acoustemology is theological reflection on how Christians know what they know in worship. Different church traditions have different acoustemologies."[31] The effectiveness of preachers depends to a significant degree on how well they employ their musical intelligence in the context of a congregation's particular acoustemology.

A church's acoustemology includes not only the music it sings and plays but also the way preachers use their voices in speaking. Effective oral communication has a music all its own. The finest preachers deliver their sermons in voices that express the sorrow and the struggle, the joy and the delight that are an integral part of the faith to which they give witness.[32] Welsh homiletics talks about the preacher's "tune," meaning not a piece of music but the unique pattern of vocal modulation that characterizes a particular preacher's delivery.[33] Good preachers have a "tune" that wins our hearts by winning our ears. Indeed, the music of speech is so essential to effective oral communication that if the tune is incongruent with the content, the tune may cancel out the intended meaning, as when, for example, a preacher declares in an angry voice that "God is love!" "Communication scholars often use the word 'paralanguage' to speak of aspects of inflection. Included in this category are such things as emphasis, loudness, and the force that is used to produce sound. In some instances, pause and rate of delivery are also classified as forms of inflection."[34] This concern for the "paralanguage" or the preacher's "tune" reveals how crucial the musical intelligence is to effective preaching. Each preacher "'needs to internalize the message so that what is communicated is both known and felt. It's not enough to write a manuscript and to read the words correctly.'"[35] A tune congruent with the gospel is what leads the heart to dance with grace.

Approaching a passage of Scripture with our musical intelligence engaged can enrich our interpretation.[36] For example, consider this passage from the Gospel of John:

"Pilate asked him [Jesus], 'What is truth?'" (John 18:38a). Read the sentence aloud. With what kind of voice do you inflect Pilate's question? Is it the off-handed voice of a busy bureaucrat who has no time for such considerations? Is it the voice of a cynic who has seen so much of power politics that he takes any talk of truth to be worthless? Is it the voice of someone who, having fought his way up through the ranks, would welcome some truth other than the dog-eat-dog world that he has always known? By being attentive to these questions of musical intelligence, we open up several sermonic possibilities including a homily that might explore three different ways of asking the question "What is truth?"

The *bodily-kinesthetic intelligence* entails
- the potential of using one's whole body
- or parts of the body (like the hand or the mouth)
- to solve problems
- or fashion products.

Preaching inescapably uses our bodily-kinesthetic intelligence: "A central fact of the preaching life is that the sight and sound of the preacher are themselves carriers of meaning. The challenge, then, for every preacher is how and in what ways to become a fully embodied communicator when preaching."[37] To become a "fully embodied communicator" is indeed a challenge, particularly for beginning preachers. People who are perfectly comfortable in their bodies as they carry on everyday tasks and conversations often freeze with nervousness and fear when they first stand to preach. They sometimes overcompensate by "choreographing movements and pauses. This, however, tends to look artificial and mechanical, creating extraneous nonverbal distraction instead of reinforcement for the sermon."[38] The very fact that preacher and congregation are aware of these realities is evidence of how important the bodily-kinesthetic intelligence is to effective communication. When the posture, gestures, and facial expression of preachers are of one piece with the content of their sermons, we sense that they are giving all of themselves to all of God, and we are drawn to doing the same.

Although the choreography of gestures is generally not effective in preaching, the use of the body in interpreting a biblical passage may reveal homiletical possibilities. Consider, for example, the woman who "had been suffering from hemorrhages for twelve years" and who in a crowd came up behind Jesus "and touched the fringe of his clothes, and immediately her hemorrhage stopped" (Luke 8:43, 44). Put yourself bodily in the scene.

You are the woman.
You are in the crowd where many people press in on Jesus.
You are feeling the pressure of the other bodies around you.
You reach out your hand toward his robe.
Stop the action just before your fingers touch the fabric.
Keep your hand extended.
Hear, see, sense, smell the crowd about you.
What do you feel in your body?
Now resume the action.

Continue the story, stopping the action whenever there is a significant change in posture and gesture.

Now review what happened with your body at each stage of the story. Let your language unfold from the bodily experience. Draw from what your body knows to articulate the process of healing. You are using the bodily-kinesthetic intelligence by engaging your body to solve the problem of interpreting the text and fashioning a sermon. If in the act of delivering the sermon you re-experience the text in the same manner, your gestures will flow naturally and be congruent with the words you speak. Gesture and language will work in concert to engage the bodily-kinesthetic intelligence of your congregation.

The *spatial intelligence* features
• the potential to recognize and manipulate the patterns of wide space (those used, for instance, by navigators and pilots)
• as well as patterns of more confined areas (such as those of importance to sculptors, surgeons, chess players, graphic artists, or architects).

Places of worship, the arrangement of their symbols, and where and how the congregation and leaders move in the course of a service all engage the spatial intelligence. Having been guest preachers in scores of different worship settings, we are aware of the immense variations in the uses of space that characterize different traditions and congregations. As newcomers we find ourselves asking questions whose answers are taken for granted by the regulars: from what door do we enter the nave or sanctuary? Where do we sit? When do we stand or bow or kneel? Do we deliver the homily from the pulpit or the chancel steps or the floor of the nave? All of these concerns and more make it impossible to ignore the spatial intelligence when we consider the worship service as a whole. But what about the sermon itself, how can we engage the spatial intelligence while we preach?

We opened this chapter with the story of a preacher artist who used her talent for drawing to bring order, coherence, and vividness to her preaching. Whether or not you are a skilled professional artist, drawing a picture of a biblical story on which you are going to base a sermon or finding a picture of it and describing it in your sermon are simple ways that you can engage your spatial intelligence as well as the congregation's.

However, you do not have to limit yourself to something that you literally see with your eyes. Many biblical passages use space in dramatic ways. When you read a story you can ask: Where are the different characters physically located? What can they see and hear? What can they not see and hear? Who moves, who stands still? Consider, for example, the healing of the paralytic as recorded in Mark 2:1-12 and Luke 5:17-26.[39] Although there are variations in the details of the narrative, both accounts agree that the crowd was so large that the paralytic's friends could not bring him directly to Jesus. They climbed up on the roof and lowered him to Jesus. Rather than race through these details, our spatial intelligence suggests ways to develop these observations about the crowd. When there is a crowd, there are people who are up front, some in the middle, and some in the rear. The ones farthest off are frequently shifting on their feet and craning their necks to hear and see what is going on. Imagine yourself among the crowd in the story. There are some people who press forward and get as close to Jesus as they can, but there are others who hold back, not yet certain they want to get too close. Where are you?

Next consider the response of the paralytic and his friends when they arrive only to discover the crowd is blocking the way. How do they get around the crowd and up onto the roof? If you are someone at the rear of the crowd and you see the paralytic and his friends digging up the roof (Mark) or lowering him through the tiles (Luke), what is your response? If you are someone at the very front of the crowd and see the man lowered directly in front of you, how do you react? How might your understanding of the entire event be shaped by your spatial relationship to Jesus, whether you are very close to him or far distant?

If you are the paralytic and you are being lowered down to Jesus, what do you see as you pass from the roof down to the floor in front of Jesus? Are you looking up through the hole in the roof or down toward the floor where you are being lowered?

Now take that same list of questions and your answers, and go to the pulpit or chancel area or stage from which you will preach the sermon. How might you use the space in which you stand as if it were the setting where the biblical story happens anew? This does not have to be melodramatic. You do not have to put on a costume or become an actor. As a matter of fact, in most cases nothing is more effective than what you set off in people's imaginations by evocative description and simple gesture. A single step forward when you talk about the crowd members who are up front, and a single step back when describing those in the rear can suggest the different spatial perspectives. Reaching and looking over the edge of the pulpit can convey the man being lowered through the roof down into the room. These are easy things to do that will engage the congregation's spatial intelligence and help them picture the story more vividly in their minds. You are carrying on an art familiar to many an African American preacher who tells biblical stories "as if one had seen them."[40] In the act of telling the story, you are seeing it yourself and thus enabling the entire congregation to see it.

The *interpersonal intelligence* denotes a person's capacity
• to understand the intentions, motivations, and desires of other people
• and, consequently, to work effectively with others.

Pastors spend an immense amount of time in exercising the interpersonal intelligence. Their role demands it. Day after day they listen to others and sense through language, behavior, vocal inflection, and body language the complexity of what moves people to feel, think, believe, and act as they do. This wisdom is essential to the preparation and presentation of sermons. Just as priests and ministers think carefully about what words someone can or cannot receive in a pastoral conversation, so too they consider what a congregation is able to hear in a sermon. Our interpersonal intelligence helps us recognize those times when a congregation is not ready for a particular word.

Christ models the restraint that arises from a keen interpersonal intelligence. He tells his disciples, " 'I still have many things to say to you, but you cannot bear them now'" (John 16:12). The Greek word for *bear* [*bastazo*] can be translated many ways—"take up," "carry," "endure." The same word is used for carrying objects, such as a jug of water (Mark 14:13) or a coffin (Luke 7:14). The muscular strength evoked by these physical meanings of the word suggests the material weight of the words that Jesus is withholding from the disciples. They are words too heavy for them to carry, too heavy for their hearts to bear, too heavy for their bodies to support. Thus the Spirit may work through our interpersonal intelligence to say to a preacher about a particular message: "Not now, later." But when the time is ripe, then our interpersonal intelligence will help us shape what we are called to speak so that it can be received even if debated and resisted.

The interpersonal intelligence is a lens for understanding many passages in the Bible. For example, the apostle Paul often begins his letters with interpersonal comments rather than launching at once into his sermons about unity, love, faith, hope, grace, baptism, and the meaning of the Lord's supper. Before he gets to the theological issues, Paul offers salutations and observations that capture the complexity of his reader's lives.

He establishes (or re-establishes) his interpersonal relationship to a congregation, and then explores how they are to work effectively with one another in ways that are faithful to the gospel. Paul ranges from affirmation to criticism in a few short verses: "I give thanks to my God always for you because of the grace of God that has been given you in Christ Jesus, for in every way you have been enriched in him, in speech and knowledge of every kind.... Now I appeal to you, brothers and sisters, by the name of our Lord Jesus Christ, that all of you be in agreement and that there be no divisions among you, but that you be united in the same mind and the same purpose" (1 Corinthians 1:4, 5-10).

In recent years we have found many preachers who avoid preaching on Paul because he seems too dry and abstract for contemporary listeners. However, if we bring our interpersonal intelligence to reading Paul, his letters become lively human documents about congregations struggling with many of the issues that confront us in our own age: How do we live as pluralistic communities? How do we honor one another's gifts? How do we deal with differences of class, race, and culture? Paul uses his interpersonal intelligence to engage the interpersonal intelligence of his readers and hearers so that by the grace of Christ they may together live a life of faith, hope, and love.

The Gospel writers are similarly attentive in portraying how Jesus interacts with others. Consider, for example, the exchange between the lawyer and Jesus that introduces and concludes the good Samaritan story. Luke pictures Jesus using his interpersonal intelligence to reframe how the man perceives and responds to the world.

"Wanting to justify himself," the lawyer asks Jesus, "'And who is my neighbor?'" (Luke 10:29). If Jesus were to point out the lawyer's desire for self-justification, the man would likely become self-defensive. Instead, Jesus employs a more indirect form of communication.[41] He tells a story and finishes by turning the lawyer's question around: "'Which of these three, do you think, was a neighbor to the man who fell into the hands of the robbers?' He said, 'The one who showed him mercy.' Jesus said to him, 'Go and do likewise.'" (Luke 10:36-37).

Jesus does not give a dictionary definition of the word *neighbor*. A definition would be restrictive: when we encounter people who fill the definition, then we would love them. Furthermore, since the man is a lawyer, he is probably adept at arguing about definitions and refining them with various exclusions and provisions. If Jesus gets into the definition game, it will become a legal contest. Instead, Jesus expands the lawyer's and our interpersonal intelligence to be more generous and gracious: we are to be neighbors to others. Jesus helps us work more effectively with one another by exercising his own interpersonal intelligence, using a story and redefining the question rather than taking on directly the lawyer's impulse for self-justification.

Redirection is a recurring pattern in the Gospels between Jesus and those who oppose him or ask him difficult questions. Instead of getting caught in webs of unsolvable disagreement, he provides a response that opens the possibility of perceiving and responding to the world in a way we had not considered before. The evangelists picture him as someone who uses his interpersonal intelligence to keep us creatively using all our many ways of knowing.

The *intrapersonal intelligence* involves
- the capacity to understand oneself,
- the capacity to have an effective working model of oneself—including one's own desires, fears, and capacities,
- the capacity to use such information effectively in regulating one's life.

The best sermons preachers preach are to themselves, not *about* themselves but *to* themselves, to the depths of their humanity, to their most intense and urgent questions about the meaning of life in face of terrible suffering, about the faith they have in God that empowers them to survive and more than survive—to be strengthened by the Spirit for redemptive work in the world.

It was a colleague in pastoral care, James B. Ashbrook, who first told me (Tom) that the best sermons are those that preachers preach *to* themselves, not *about* themselves.[42] Now, after more than thirty years of teaching homiletics and listening to hundreds of experienced pastors in workshops or their own pulpits, I can confirm the truth of Ashbrook's observation.

The distinction between a sermon *to* oneself and *about* oneself is significant, and Gardner's three-part definition of the intrapersonal intelligence clarifies why a sermon to oneself is much more effective for the congregation than a sermon about oneself.

When we preach about ourselves, the focus is on us. We are what the sermon is about. A sermon about ourselves reveals us struggling to develop the first characteristic of Gardner's intrapersonal intelligence: the capacity to understand ourselves. It is a struggle worthy of a conversation with our best friend or trusted counselor, but it does not belong in the pulpit.

By way of contrast, a sermon to ourselves reveals that we have the capacity to understand ourselves, and that we have an effective working model of ourselves—including our own desires, fears, and capacities

(Gardner's second characteristic). We know firsthand the dreams that wake us in the night, the anxieties that haunt us, the wrestling matches between our doubt and our faith, the griefs and grudges that choke our best efforts at being gracious, the insatiable hunger for an assurance that keeps eluding the reach of our heart, and the imperfect and often ineffective strategies we employ for keeping all of these forces from overwhelming us. In knowing these things we know what it is to be a human being. When our sermons address the reality of our humanness, they resonate with other human beings, with their hunger and yearning, their fear and their hope. When we preach to ourselves, the focus is not on us but on what the word of God or the risen Christ or the living Spirit has to say to us. The congregation learns less about us and more about how God reaches to human beings at the level of their deepest need.

A sermon preached to oneself may or may not include direct reference to the preacher. Sometimes there will be a story out of the preacher's life, but often not. The principle here is that the sermon is addressed to the human situation of the preacher rather than the preacher's idiosyncrasies, and the sermon therefore speaks to the human situation of the congregation. Such sermons supply theological substance that preachers have tested in the fierce crucible of their own hearts and have found to be true and much larger than themselves.

We think here of two sermons by two different preachers: one was *about* the preacher, and the other *to* the preacher. Both sermons were on forgiveness. The sermon *about* the preacher recounted one painfully revealing family story after another. The congregation looked on as spectators rather than participants.

The other sermon was preached by someone whose spouse had been murdered. But the preacher's story did not dominate the sermon. Instead, the story drew us into an exploration of what is involved in the struggle to forgive: the adrenaline of rage, the sustaining energies of hatred that over time turn corrosive, the first hints of grace and peace and the preacher's resistance to them, the oscillation between hanging on and letting go the bitterness, and finally a vision of hope not yet attained but beckoning and supplying courage for the future. The sermon addressed the preacher's human situation with such honesty and theological insight that it did the same for the congregation. Afterward, we had a transforming conversation about the strenuous, long-term process of realizing God's grace in our bitterly fragmented world. The preacher's intrapersonal intelligence had created a powerful sermon in the congregation by using the preacher's humanity to awaken the common humanity of us all.

The *naturalist intelligence* involves
• expertise in the recognition and classification of the numerous species—the flora and fauna—of his or her environment.

Because the Scriptures were written before the development of modern science, it is easy to think that of all the eight intelligences in MI theory the naturalist intelligence is perhaps the one that preachers are least likely to develop. However, there are several reasons for engaging this intelligence in our sermons.

First of all, even though the biblical writers do not describe the natural world using the taxonomies of modern scientists, they are often acutely observant about seasons, plants, and animals. For example, mark the precision with which the psalmist describes his environment in the context of a hymn of thanksgiving and praise to God the Creator:

> The trees of the LORD are watered abundantly,
> the cedars of Lebanon that he planted.
> In them the birds build their nests;
> the stork has its home in the fir trees.
> The high mountains are for the wild goats;
> the rocks are a refuge for the coneys. (Psalm 104:16-18)

A preacher whose naturalist intelligence is engaged will ask what a coney is [sometimes spelled "cony"]. Working our way through an American language dictionary and then a biblical dictionary we found a scientific description of the creature under the heading "Rock Badger." The psalmist is referring to "any of a family of small ungulate mammals, the hyraxes, of which *ca.* fourteen species are known. The only variety found outside Africa is the Syrian hyrax (*procavia syriaca*). Except for its inconspicuous ears, the appearance of the hyrax is like that of the rabbit, which it also resembles in size. Unlike the rabbit, it does not burrow but lives in rocky regions."[43] Bless the Lord, O my soul, for the ungulate mammals, for the hyraxes, for the *procavia syriaca*, rabbit-like but with inconspicuous ears and living among the rocks! The scientific language will reach listeners who perceive and process the world through their naturalist intelligence.

Blending such language with the biblical idiom does something more: it helps overcome the perception of some people that religious faith and science are antithetical to each other. To praise God for the ungulate mammals, including the *procavia syriaca*, vivifies and deepens the sense of wonder expressed by the psalmist. It encourages us to celebrate the accomplishments of science while keeping us humble about all human knowledge by placing it in the context of God's creative work. Our homiletical use of the naturalist intelligence nurtures a dialogue between science and theology: science provides ever-increasing knowledge of how the natural environment functions, while theology sustains our sense of responsibility for how we treat the creation that belongs to God and not to us. Thus the sermonic engagement of the naturalist intelligence has an environmental, ethical dimension. We employ this intelligence in our homilies not only to communicate with more of the congregation, but to nurture the faithful stewardship of the ecosystem of planet earth.

USING MI THEORY TO REACH THE WHOLE BODY OF CHRIST

Asking people to respond to sermons without giving them any tools for analysis is often frustrating for preachers and listeners alike.[44] Because sermons are usually delivered in a holy place and in the context of worship, and because people respect their pastor, it is often difficult for them to speak in helpful, critical ways about what they have heard. However, if we provide them usable tools, and if we make it clear that we are interested not simply in the sermon we delivered, but the sermon they created from what we delivered (see the material on Reuel Howe earlier in this chapter), then the conversation can be mutually illuminating.

We have discovered that teaching listeners the basic elements of MI theory can make them more articulate about how and why preachers are actively engaging or failing to engage their participation. Here is an exercise to introduce MI theory that you can do with a study group that helps you prepare sermons or with your ruling board or even with the whole congregation in the course of delivering a sermon. We suggest you begin by reading the two greatest commandments in Mark 12:28-31 and portions of 1 Corinthians 12:4-30, which opens with the observation "Now there are varieties of gifts, but the same Spirit; and there are varieties of services, but the same Lord; and there are varieties of activities, but it is the same God who activates all of them in everyone." You can then introduce MI theory as a way of engaging all of us for all of God and honoring the various gifts that are found in the Body of Christ, among the whole congregation.

Ask them: "By a show of hands, how many of you think you're intelligent?" Then say, "Even if you did not raise your hand, all of you are intelligent, and not in just one or two ways. Each of us has the potential to be intelligent in eight different ways. Eight—that's right, I said eight ways of being intelligent, eight different ways of being smart. We say of people who are knowledgeable and competent about what they do in life: 'They have a lot of smarts.' The fact of the matter is that God has given us all a lot of smarts."

Now proceed through the eight intelligences in the following way:[45]

"How many of you can speak? How many can write? How many read the service leaflet? In order to speak, write, and read you have to use words, so all of you are Word Smart.

"How many of you tried to figure out what you had to do to get here on time today? How many weighed your options about what to do after we are finished? In order to do any of that you have to use some form of logic, so you are Logic Smart.

"How many of you like to see videos, movies, pictures, or stained glass windows in a church? That indicates you are Picture Smart.

48

"How many of you like to stand to sing, walk, move around, make things with your hands, play sports? Then you are Body Smart.

"How many of you enjoy singing in the congregation or listening to our choir and instrumentalists or hearing birds chirp, the wind blowing through the trees, and waves lapping at the shore? If you do, you are Music Smart.

"How many of you have at least one friend or enjoy being with a family member or talking with someone during church? Then you are People Smart.

"How many of you like to work alone some of the time or go to some special place inside yourself or somewhere else or pray quietly before and during worship? Then you are Self Smart.

"How many of you enjoy being out in nature or have pets or like to see the flowers in church? Then you are Nature Smart."

If you use PowerPoint, you might project appropriate images for each of the intelligences or "smarts." Or instead of PowerPoint, you might use posters. Once you have gone through the eight questions, explain Gardner's theory and relate these "smarts" to living more faithfully the greatest commandments and realizing more completely what it is to be the Body of Christ, a community of many gifts. MI theory helps us embody these spiritual realities by honoring the fullness and uniqueness of human ways of knowing. Each person has a particular blend of these intelligences. Each is stronger in some and weaker in others. We all have the potential for using any of the eight intelligences, but we are not the same. For example, an interest in the musical intelligence does not automatically make us an accomplished musical artist. But by honoring all eight intelligences we honor interests as well as highly developed skills. Someone might not be an environmentalist, but may follow popular articles on the subject written for laypeople, and when we engage that intelligence in our sermons we engage that person's interest.

Explain to the group how you as a preacher want to enhance the richness of communication in your sermons by more frequently drawing upon all the intelligences so that you reach the whole person and the whole congregation. Invite them to participate in the process. To help them, you can supply copies of the following chart on which they can note when and how you engaged a particular intelligence.

MULTIPLE INTELLIGENCES CHART

Linguistic (Word Smart)	Logical-mathematical (Logic Smart)	Musical (Music Smart)	Bodily-kinesthetic (Body Smart)
• Sensitivity to spoken and written language • Ability to learn languages • Capacity to use language to accomplish certain goals	• Capacity to analyze problems logically • Capacity to carry out mathematical operations • Capacity to investigate issues scientifically	• Skill in performance • Skill in composition • Skill in appreciation for musical patterns	• Potential to use one's whole body • Potential to use parts of the body (e.g., hand) • Potential to solve problems • Potential to fashion products

Spatial (Picture Smart)	Interpersonal (People Smart)	Intrapersonal (Self Smart)	Naturalist (Nature Smart)
• Potential to recognize and manipulate patterns of wide space (e.g., pilots) • Potential to recognize and manipulate patterns of more confined space (e.g., sculptors, architects)	• Ability to understand the intentions, motivations, and desires of other people • Ability to work effectively with others	• Capacity to understand oneself • Capacty to have an effective working model of oneself • Capacity to regulate one's life effectively	• Potential to recognize and classify numerous species of flora and fauna

Do not have them fill out the chart while you are preaching, but afterward. Then when they come together to discuss the sermon with you, have everybody share their charts. In some cases different people will pick up different intelligences because their patterns of response may favor one intelligence over the other. We tend to be more alert to the intelligences that are most highly developed in ourselves. This is important to know, not only for you the preacher but for the whole congregation, because it reveals the plurality of different gifts in the community. It helps the congregation understand your need to say things in many different ways and their need to honor the different ways of knowing that are operating among themselves. In this way, the use of MI theory becomes a way not only of enhancing your preaching but of more fully realizing Paul's vision of a church that values all the members of Christ's Body.

Like any other theory, MI is not an end in itself, and we do not suggest that you use the MI chart for every sermon! Yet, we have found MI extremely helpful for implementing our vision of preaching to the whole congregation. How can we preach so that we engage all of the various intelligences? That question directs preaching to be person-centered, as well as message-centered, so that we seek to know and to respect each individual within our congregations.

MI AND SERMON PREPARATION

Multiple Intelligences theory expands our understanding of the modes of human learning. Some preachers, because their own verbal intelligence is so highly developed, presuppose that people prefer a hearing style of learning. In our experience some people learn more by seeing. Others prefer to learn by doing, especially young children. Certainly preaching involves talking and making logical connections, but MI suggests we can also involve congregations in seeing images, singing songs, using gestures (dancing?), exchanging comments, exploring their feelings, or appreciating a floral arrangement. Henry Mitchell has written a highly balanced assessment of the place of reason [the logical-mathematical intelligence] in preaching. He names six essential functions for reason: making sense, monitoring, achieving a reasonable sequence of words, coherence, motivating the listening process, and linking what is preached to real life applications. But having established why reason is essential, Mitchell observes how reason alone is inadequate.[46] There is a need to engage the whole person. Hence we consider the possibilities of blending the four modes of learning that we named in chapter 1—thinking, feeling, imagining, and doing—with all eight intelligences in MI theory.[47]

Can you imagine eight ways to stimulate thinking about justice through a sermon?

Eight ways to evoke feelings about reconciliation?

Eight ways to fire the imagination about being an inclusive church?

Eight ways to practice stewardship?

At first these questions may seem overwhelming, but MI theory makes answering them much more doable because it breaks the process down into a number of discrete operations that provide us multiple ways to approach our task. Consider, for example, how we might use MI theory to prepare a sermon on Luke 15:1-7. In this text, a narrative setting (15:1-3) provides the reason for Jesus to tell a parable (15:4-6) that Jesus compares with subject matter introduced in the narrative setting (15:7).

1 Now all the tax collectors and sinners were coming near to listen to him. [2]And the Pharisees and the scribes were grumbling and saying, "This fellow welcomes sinners and eats with them."
3 So he told them this parable: [4]"Which one of you, having a hundred sheep and losing one of them, does not leave the ninety-nine in the wilderness and go after the one that is lost until he finds it? [5]When he has found it, he lays it on his shoulders and rejoices. [6]And when he comes home, he calls together his friends and neighbors, saying to them, 'Rejoice with me, for I have found my sheep that was lost.' [7]Just so, I tell you, there will be more joy in heaven over one sinner who repents than over ninety-nine righteous persons who need no repentance."

Using the eight intelligences, we could brainstorm with our sermon preparation group or with ourselves how each intelligence might relate to this text. We start with the naturalist intelligence—nature smart—and conclude with verbal intelligence—word smart—for two reasons: one, we cannot avoid using words since this will be a sermon, and two, by engaging the other intelligences first we are more apt to awaken fresh insight and vivid language.

Do not simply scan through this list. Take time to respond to what arises as you engage each intelligence.

Nature Smart:
Wilderness can be terrifying.
Have you ever been lost in a wilderness?

Self Smart:
What did the shepherd feel about the lost sheep?
What is most valuable for you?

People Smart:
Jesus welcomes sinners and the shepherd joins friends.
Is this story a parable about the mission of the church for "outsiders"?

Music Smart:
Hear the Pharisees "grumble."
Hear the shepherd rejoice with his friends.
Sing "Amazing Grace."

Body Smart:
The shepherd seeks, finds, puts the sheep on his shoulders, and calls to friends.
Imagine the weight of the sheep on your shoulders.
Does the sheep squirm?
What do you have to do to keep the sheep from falling off?
Faith is embodied in what we do as much as in what we are.

Picture Smart:

Jesus responds to the grumbling with a picture parable.

I can see the shepherd searching as an image of our searching for what we may have lost in life.

How do you see it?

Logic Smart:

It does not make sense to leave the ninety-nine in the wilderness unprotected.

Have you ever thought about how irrational Christian faith really is?

Why do we proclaim that God is love but face all sorts of evil in the world?

Word Smart:

Jesus' parable (word) confronts the exclusive rationality of the Pharisees.

What parable might we speak to confront the exclusive rationalities of our world today?

Notice that the deliberate engagement of each intelligence often makes us attentive to details we missed. For example, using our nature smarts alerted us to the wilderness in the passage, something that initially escaped our notice. Go back through the exercise and ask yourself, What occurred to you as a result of using the multiple intelligences that you might otherwise have missed? This is more than an exercise. It is a form of spiritual discipline, a way of magnifying our attentiveness and responsiveness to the Word of God. It is a way of engaging all the ways of knowing that God has given us so that we can engage all the ways of knowing that God has given to the congregation. It is a way of growing in the love and the knowledge of God.

Preaching and Children's Ways of Knowing

And a Little Child Shall Lead Them[1]

A student told this story in class about her little daughter. I (Tom) do not recall the child's name, but I will call her Susan. The week after Christmas, while they were driving to an appointment, Susan asked her mother to stop at their church and see how the baby Jesus was doing. She had attended the Christmas pageant and remembered seeing baby Jesus in the manger. She wanted to make sure he was OK and getting well fed. The mother, knowing they needed to press ahead to the appointment, tried to explain it was a pageant that Susan had seen, and that the baby Jesus by now had been put away in the church storage room until next year. This alarmed the child. She wondered who would feed baby Jesus in the storage room. The mother persisted in trying to explain that "it was only a play," but Susan only became more adamant that the baby needed food. The mother, knowing they had no time to stop at church, suddenly realized that adult explanations would not break through to her child. Instead of trying to explain that the pageant was a play, she entered her daughter's world and said that the shepherds would make sure the baby Jesus was fed. This made excellent sense to Susan, who was then willing to ride on to the appointment knowing that someone was caring for the baby Jesus.

The story illustrates a phenomenon that experts in children's ways of knowing have documented. Young children live in a magical world full of both wonder and fear. They have not yet developed the conceptual capacities to understand the difference between a pageant and real life, between a symbol and an idea. As far as the little girl was concerned, baby Jesus had literally been born in that church. Susan had seen the infant with her own eyes, and no amount of adult explanation was going to alter the reality of that simple fact.

Before we conclude that Susan's perception is naive and immature, and before we dismiss the incident as nothing more than a cute story, we need to consider the power of the little girl's conviction. Her way of knowing leads the child to raise a question that we adults, with all of our sophisticated conceptual abilities, may have ignored: who will feed the baby Jesus? The bluntness of the girl's concern compels us to come to terms with the ethical implications of Christ's birth. What Isaiah prophesied becomes true: "A little child shall lead them" (Isaiah 11:6). Through her child's way of perceiving and responding to the world the little girl leads us to a profound insight into the meaning of Christ's birth.

Susan's story reveals why we adults love to watch the children in church during Christmas: the children put us back in touch with a world of wonder, and they reawaken perceptual capacities that have been dulled by the burden of our adult lives.

Nevertheless, the child's perception alone is not enough. Who will feed the baby Jesus? Any adequate response demands adult reasoning and action. We will have to consider how Christ is to be found among the hungry children of the world. We will have to analyze the systems of food production and delivery. We will have to formulate economic and political strategies that make sure the children receive the nutrition and care that are essential to growing up healthy and strong.

We honor children when we take seriously their ways of knowing that are not burdened with all of our adult distinctions and abstractions. Children often awaken us to elemental realities we have neglected: someone needs to feed Jesus. We are not talking about becoming naive[2] or sentimental, but rather about enriching our ways of perceiving and responding to the world so that we benefit from the wisdom children have to offer the whole community. We do not romanticize children. Like us adults, they can be bad and wrongheaded, but they can also be good and insightful, and their ways of knowing are as important to the community of faith as adult ways. Furthermore, "Children face daily situations that are as challenging as those that are faced by adults. They need to hear about God's love and forgiveness, and think with the rest of the congregation about what it means to be among God's people. We have a responsibility to preach to the kids as well as sing and pray with them."[3]

In this chapter we will explore how preachers can draw upon children's ways of knowing to create and deliver sermons that are not children's sermons but that engage children and adults at the same time. (Yes, it is possible to do this!) Then in the next chapter we will consider adult perspectives that can enrich our preaching even more. The two chapters together place preaching in the context of the entire life cycle. We believe this intergenerational vision is essential in order for preaching to be faithful to God, whose love and grace extend to people of every age and condition. Our communication strategy—our rhetoric—grows directly out of the gospel that affirms God's unambiguous love for infants, toddlers, children, teenagers, young adults, the middle-aged, seniors, and the very aged. A homiletical rhetoric that consistently employs only one way of knowing contradicts the good news of God's grace for all. All of us for all of God includes all generations.

We contextualize both children's and adults' ways of knowing by sharing a poem that celebrates the entire life cycle. The poem was commissioned by a woman whose mother had been a very great teacher. Her daughter had subsequently developed an intense commitment to education, including Christian education in the church. She wanted a poem that her church musician, a gifted composer, could set as a choir anthem and that could be used in churches whenever they celebrated their educational ministries. Although she asked for the poem to be written specifically about teaching, we believe it applies equally to preaching.

We invite you to substitute the word *preachers* for *teachers*, a move that fits well with Clark Williamson's and Ronald Allen's proposal that preachers view "every sermon to an established congregation as a teaching event."[4]

> Infant child,
> you gaze around
> at all things new.
> You babble, wail,
> you smile and coo
> and trust the world
> will answer you.
>
> Thanks be to God for teachers
> who nurture what the child makes clear:
> that learning springs from trust, not fear.
>
> Little one,
> you stand, you step,
> you fall down boom.
> You stand, you step,
> you fall down boom.
> You stand, you step,
> you cross the room!
>
> Thanks be to God for teachers
> who trust the wisdom toddlers know:
> we all fall down to learn and grow.
>
> Playful child,
> you run, you skip
> you leap up high.
> You flap yours arms,
> you want to fly
> and touch the stars
> that fill the sky.

Thanks be to God for teachers
who help creative thinking spring
from children's wild imagining.

Searching youth,
you snap the ties
that childhood weaves;
the magic world
the eye perceives,
the simple creed the heart believes.

Thanks be to God for teachers
who honor what the youth attest:
that doubt as well as faith is blest.

Young adult,
you hope the good
your heart intends
survives the times
life's road descends
through tangled wood
to unmapped ends.

Thanks be to God for teachers,
who ready both the mind and heart
for worlds the present cannot chart.

Middle aged,
you live between
your children's cries
and parent's needs,
and when you rise
you pray that God
will make you wise.

Thanks be to God for teachers
who guide a soul in how to weigh
the dawn and dying of the day.

Rich in years,
your heart still leaps
at birds in flight
but now by faith
you stretch your sight
beyond the stars
that fill the night.

Thanks be to God for teachers
who by their lives this faith have sown:
one day we'll know as we are known.[5]

BECOMING CONVERSANT WITH CHILDREN'S WAYS OF KNOWING

Did little Susan who wanted to feed the infant Jesus keep alive her compassionate faith while developing her powers of adult reasoning and action? We do not know. The mother told the story many years ago. By now her daughter is an adult. We hope the child grew up following the pattern of Jesus' own maturation as described by Luke: "And Jesus increased in wisdom and in years, and in divine and human favor" (Luke 2:52). The chances of Susan having achieved that goal are much greater if her childlike ways of knowing were taken seriously by her community of faith, including the preachers she heard. When sermons include children's ways of knowing, they become more effective in providing Christian nurture to every generation of listener. Reconnecting to these ways of perceiving and responding is an important pastoral art. We say "reconnecting" because all of us once upon a time were children. If growing up involved the total loss of these childhood capacities, then our adult observation of them in children would not have such deep resonance in our hearts. When a child cries out in the night that a monster is in the room, we recall the ghosts and demons that woke us up when we were little. When a child insists that she saw Jesus born in church, we glimpse again the wonder that used to fill us during the Christmas pageant. The memories are in us. Nevertheless, it takes imaginative work to become an adult who is conversant with children's ways of knowing.

When I (Tom) was a child my father measured my two brothers and me every few months. He would mark our name, our height, and the date of the measurement on a piece of white painted woodwork between the kitchen and the pantry. I used to look at those marks and marvel at how much I had grown. I would sometimes bend my knees in order to lower my head to a mark made one or two years earlier. Could it really be that I once was that short? Next I would stand up straight, and then on my tip toes try to imagine where I might be a year into the future.

I wonder how Mary and Joseph marked Jesus' growth. Like most parents, they probably observed when his sleeves had become too short. But what about his spiritual growth? They evidently gave careful attention to his learning the customs and rituals of their tradition. We read in the gospel, "Now every year his parents went to Jerusalem for the festival of the Passover" (Luke 2:41). That annual celebration must have made a strong impression upon Jesus as a child, probably gripping his mind with the same power as the Christmas pageant gripped the little girl's. Since Jesus was fully human he must have progressed through the same early modes of cognition as the little girl. He might very well have asked some naive, childlike question about what the Hebrew slaves did with their chains or how many chariots were lost in the sea. As the years progressed, Jesus moved beyond his literalism toward the deeper meanings of the tradition. Luke says Jesus amazed the Temple authorities when he was twelve, an age when children begin to claim the powers of adult reasoning. Although the story of Jesus as a twelve-year-old sage in the Temple is shaped by the piety of the early church, it is possible that the story captures a memory of something that really happened.

When Christ calls, "Follow me," he calls us to grow up, to become adult believers who have hearts childlike enough to ask, "Who will feed the baby Jesus?" and who have minds keen enough to figure out what it will take, and who have wills strong enough to do it.

If you let children interpret the Bible for themselves, you can learn a lot about being childlike even while you remain an adult. Listen to children attentively, and you can become conversant in their ways of knowing. Here is a conversation we had with a six-year-old boy to whom we read the parable of the lost sheep.[6]

"'What man of you, having a hundred sheep, if he has lost one of them, does not leave the ninety-nine in the wilderness, and go after the one which is lost, until he finds it? And when he has found it, he lays it on his shoulders, rejoicing. And when he comes home, he calls together his friends and his neighbors, saying to them, "Rejoice with me, for I have found my sheep which was lost"'" (Luke 15:4-6 RSV).

I asked him: "Why do you think Jesus told that story?"

He looked puzzled and said, "I'm trying to think. I don't know. Jesus told that story?"

Failing to get another response, I tried a different question: "What was the story about?"

He answered, "It was about a lost sheep. He left all the sheep out in the wilderness—they'd run around and then he'd have to find them. He should have left them in a sort of a thing that has a fence around them so they can't get out."

I then asked, "Do you think that was a good thing, to find the lost sheep?"

He answered, "Yeah, to find the sheep but he might lose all the rest."

I asked him, "Now, why do you think Jesus told that story?"

He answered, "So people would have stupid ideas."

Nearly six years later, I reminded him of the story and began another dialogue.[7]

I asked him, "What does that mean to you?"

He responded, "The parable of the lost sheep is about when a shepherd has a hundred sheep and one of them gets lost and he has to go out and find that one sheep."

I then asked, "What do you think about that story? What do you think that story means?"

He replied, "Well that story is about, what I think is that, when that shepherd loses a sheep, he knows that that one sheep is lost and doesn't know where to go; it could be dead or dying and hurt while his other sheep are fine, and so he can just go out and find that one; he should find that one."

I said, "Why do you think Jesus told that story?"

He said, "Well, to explain to people that there may be a hundred people but if one dies you might say, 'Well, one out of a hundred really doesn't matter,' but one out of a hundred really does matter."

I was intrigued by his response, especially since he had not attended church school nor, to my knowledge, had I discussed with him this parable at any length, if at all, in the intervening years. So I asked him if he remembered what he got out of the parable several years before.

I said, "Can you remember that?"

He said, "No."

I reminded him, "You told us that you thought it was a stupid story. What do you think of that?"

He said, "Well, I was a little kid then."

I asked, "So you get something different out of it now, right?"

He concluded, "Well maybe as you get older, as you change and move around and go to different places, you see different sides of the story."

We learn a lot from these two conversations. For instance, the difference between the boy's first interpretation and the one he offered nearly six years later illustrates a change in his mode of cognition. His way of knowing or making meaning had undergone a structural transformation. He no longer interpreted what he experienced through literal and concrete cognitive capabilities: things are what they are. At twelve, he was beginning to think abstractly and to formulate hypotheses in his head. So he moved easily from the story to a simple but abstract comparative idea. He evaluated his literal interpretation as typical of "a little kid," because he now was able to come up with a deeper meaning.

The story about Susan wanting to feed the baby Jesus and the interviews with the young boy illustrate characteristics of two different ways of knowing found among children. We name these ways of knowing "Magical Maggie" and "Literal Larry." We do not attach labels to living individuals whose humanity is too complex to be reduced to one way of knowing. But we have found that personifying the different ways of knowing with alliterative names helps our students remember their distinctive characteristics.

In describing Magical Maggie and Literal Larry we write about "ways" or "modes" of knowing rather than "stages." The word *stage* in our experience is fraught with too much baggage. It suggests, at least to some people, that one way of knowing or one individual is superior to another, or that having left a stage behind, we will never use it again—neither of which is true. Each cognitive process has a contribution to make to the community of faith, and so we write about "ways of knowing" or "modes of learning" or "perspectives."[8]

In the discussion that follows, Magical Maggie and Literal Larry are heuristic devices that help us distinguish different ways of knowing. However, the children whose responses manifest these different ways of knowing are not fictional. In some cases they are children whose ways of knowing, I (Ed) documented over the course of many years as they grew up and matured.

Magical Maggie sees the world as full of wonder and fanciful, like a kaleidoscope. As she talks about her experiences she tends to mix fact and fantasy. When hearing a story, she will usually focus on one thing that fits her fancy. As a preschool perspective, Magical Maggie's way of knowing is shaped by the way things appear to her. If you smash one of two clay balls of equal size, she will say that one of them has more in it because of the way it appears to her.

Literal Larry sees the world as literal and concrete and centered in what Larry wants. When he talks about his experiences he thinks in terms of what is literally true and proven by what he can see and touch. When hearing a story, he will reproduce the narrative point by point and evaluate the parts of a story in terms of what he knows are specific concrete realities. Literal Larry knows that clay balls do not change in amount when they change size, because he has learned about the conservation of amount. Literal Larry also has the uncanny ability to classify and organize all sorts of information: baseball averages, dinosaurs, birds, trees, and so forth.[9]

ONE STORY, DIFFERENT UNDERSTANDINGS

Preaching to children often involves telling stories, particularly stories from the Bible. But different children will have different understandings of the same story. Some of them will hear the story through the perspective of Magical Maggie while others will hear it through the perspective of Literal Larry. We get the flavor of these different ways of knowing through the responses children made to the following story from Matthew: When asked if it was "'lawful to cure on the sabbath,'" Jesus replied, "'Suppose one of you has only one sheep and it falls into a pit on the sabbath; will you not lay hold of it and lift it out? How much more valuable is a human being than a sheep!'" (Matthew 12:10-11). The children were asked two questions: Should Jesus have broken the law? Which is more important or of more value, a sheep or a man?[10]

Some of the children used Magical Maggie's way of knowing:

Jesus should have broken the law "'cause Jesus is the boss."

The Pharisees were "bad, they're going to kill Jesus."

"A sheep is worth more 'cause it can make clothes. If a man could make clothes, the man and the sheep would both be worth more than a horse 'cause a horse can't make clothes.... It would depend on whether the sheep was bigger (or older) than the man."

The perspective of Magical Maggie is manifest in these responses. It centers attention on one or more striking features. The interpretations are fanciful and include a nonlinear collage of interests: sheep, clothes, man, horse! Typically for Magical Maggie, people are seen as big or little, strong or weak, good or bad, with the biggest being the "goodest." There is a value judgment based on who or what is bigger and older. Persons who make the laws and punish will appear to her as omnipotent authorities. In the Magical Maggie perspective, law is something you are not supposed to do or you will get into trouble. The oldest and biggest determine what is right.

Other children responding to the same questions about the same passage from Matthew used Literal Larry's way of knowing:

Jesus should have broken the law because "I think it is a good thing to do at least one or two good deeds on Sunday. Jesus is different. He was kind of a good guy and the Pharisees don't understand him so, well, in this case it's right to heal."

Also, the Pharisees were not justified in being upset, because "they wanted to be the big cheese, see that people obeyed the law."

"The man, cause the sheep can turn into lamb chops. . . . In them days the only things they used the sheep for was to eat and sprinkle the blood over the fence posts around the door. Well, let's see, I think they could probably do some things that a person can. I think the sheep's as important as a man, yeah."

Manifesting Literal Larry's way of knowing, these children interpret the story through concrete ways of thinking about "good" as "good deeds" and the number of things persons or animals can do. This perspective views the story as a one-dimensional narrative that refers to concrete and specific reality. Typically for Literal Larry, the interpretation is exact and exhaustive in retelling the literal details of the narrative. People are seen in terms of how useful they are to others, but also as self-centered. Persons or animals are viewed in terms of the number of things that they can do to benefit one's self and others. If people have earned recognition because of their ability they may be trusted, or they may be seen as self-serving. Laws exist to prevent harm and unfairness. What is right is based on what the person wants or who is most useful or what is fair, and fairness is defined as equal exchange.

SEEING GOD FROM THE PERSPECTIVES OF MAGICAL MAGGIE AND LITERAL LARRY

How do children see God when their ways of knowing are like Magical Maggie's and Literal Larry's? Asking children about God can be daunting to us adults, who may have strong convictions about what constitutes right or wrong doctrine. We may be anxious that the children believe "correctly." But if we enter their world without needing them to think about God as we do, children may open us to dimensions of the divine that elude our sophisticated thought.

Here are two brief interviews.

Interviewer: "What do you think God might look like?"
Girl: [*without hesitation*] "Air. You know why?"
Interviewer: "Why?"
Girl: "He's everywhere."[11]

Magical Maggie's way of knowing is evident in that God is "everywhere" and can see everything.

The second interview:

Interviewer: "What does God mean to you? Who's God?"
Boy: "Who's God?"
Interviewer: "Yeah. What's God?"
Boy: "You know what's God?"
Interviewer: "What's your idea?"
Boy: "Love."
Interviewer: "What do you mean by that?"
Boy: "God is love."
After some discussion, the interviewer asked, "What does that mean to you?"
Boy: "Buddies."
Interviewer: "Buddies? So God is a buddy?"

Boy: "No. He's love. God is love."
Interviewer: "All right, where did you learn that?"
Boy: "I just thought it up."[12]

This interpretation has the concreteness that is typical of Literal Larry's perspective. God is love means "buddies" to the child. Further conversation reveals that his concrete way of knowing extends to picturing God in human form, living in heaven, and rewarding and punishing people in specific ways.

A CHART AND A LIST FOR PREACHING TO MAGICAL MAGGIE AND LITERAL LARRY

Below you will find a summary chart of some of the distinguishing features of these two ways of knowing. You can use the chart as a checklist when preparing a sermon for the perspectives of Magical Maggie or Literal Larry. You can also use the chart to evaluate a sermon you preached or have heard, and to understand children whose ways of knowing and expressing themselves are reflected here.

Subject/Areas of Thought	Magical Maggie	Literal Larry
World	Magical, mixes fact & fancy	Concrete, literal
Logic	Magical appearance	Literally true, concrete, conservation, classification
Story	Striking feature	Narrative, one dimensional, literal

Persons	Big or little, strong or weak, good or bad	Usefulness, self-centered
Value of Life	Bigger and older more value	Number of abilities
Law	Do what the law says or get in trouble	Prevent concrete acts of harm
Authority	Located in biggest, the boss	Located in persons with abilities
Right	What the oldest and biggest say	What I want, gets rewards, fair
God	Everywhere, sees everything	Human form, punishes and awards specific people

Because you, the readers of this book, also have different ways of processing and knowing, it may be helpful to have this information in another form. Therefore, we provide below a simple listing of the characteristics of Magical Maggie's and Literal Larry's ways of knowing. Some people think in charts, others think in lists. Human ways of knowing are indeed varied!

Magical Maggie:	**Literal Larry:**
Mixes fact and fancy	Concrete/literal
Objects appear to be	Things are proven concretely
Big/little	Classifies
Good/bad	Who is useful to me
Strong/weak	What is fair/unfair
Ego-centric	Who/what gets rewards
Do what the law says to keep out	Numbers of abilities
of trouble	Law prevents destructive acts
The oldest/biggest is the boss	and unfairness
A symbol is the same as its	Symbol refers to specific
representation	concrete reality
Focus on striking persons/	Literal narratives in Bible
objects in Bible	God is in human form
God is everywhere	

A SAMPLE SERMON WITH ANALYSIS

We now turn to a sermon that uses children's ways of knowing, especially that of Literal Larry. The sermon is not intended for children alone. The concreteness of the language and the vividness of the story line are close to the spirit of Jesus' parables and, like his parables, can engage both children and adults while evoking multiple meanings in the congregation. As Gene Lowry has observed, "The storyteller or parable preacher does not have to produce such connections of meaning; life does."[13] The sermon uses children's ways of knowing to engage the adult ways of knowing that we will discuss in the next chapter. The concreteness of this homiletical method, the gift of Literal Larry, speaks directly to children while it awakens metaphorical and conceptual thought in adults. The sermon demonstrates a form of parabolic preaching that all generations can understand.

The sermon is based on a miracle story (John 6:1-14), the feeding of the five thousand. Although we think of parables and miracles as different genres, that is a highly adult distinction requiring a form of logical reasoning that a child has not yet developed. By moving into the child's world and idiom, we become less focused on such conceptual distinctions. We open ourselves to wonder and belief, a wonder and belief that revitalize our trust in Jesus' parables of grace.

Because I (Tom) preached this sermon originally to a congregation that included many highly intellectual adults, there is a brief interlude after the opening exchange that employs adult reasoning. Also, the mother throughout the sermon gives voice to adult reasoning without taking over the sermon. I felt this was necessary in order to justify a homiletical strategy that might awaken some resistance in such a sophisticated congregation.

We have annotated the sermon with parenthetical comments that identify characteristics of children's ways of knowing. Since parabolic preaching also uses language that evokes response from our multiple intelligences, we suggest those possible connections in bold type.[14] Thus the sermon and the annotations will help you to see two theories of knowing working together in concert: both **multiple intelligences theory**

(MI) in bold print and (children's ways of knowing in parentheses). We suggest that you read the sermon aloud, inflecting the voices of mother and child so that you get some idea of how the sermon is **Music Smart** through its attention to the melody of human speech.

THE SERMON

"Isaiah. Isaaaaaiah!
You didn't eat the lunch
I packed for you."

The use of a parent's vocal inflection is music smart.

"Yes, I did, Mom.
Honest.
I ate the whole thing."

(This typical parent-child exchange brackets the preacher's explanatory comments to the adult congregation.)
Here and throughout the dialogues the sermon is Word Smart and People Smart.

Actually,
we don't know what the boy's name was.
The Gospel of John
never tells us.
John simply calls him a boy
who has five barley loaves and two fish.

But I want to consider
this whole story
of the feeding of the five thousand
from the boy's perspective.

71

I am not satisfied calling him
"the boy."
It is always tempting for us adults to do that,
to forget the full humanity of children.
I will call him Isaiah.

Isaiah seems a fine name for the youngster,
especially since
it was the prophet Isaiah
who taught that
"a little child shall lead them,"
a teaching that seems
to find an echo
in Jesus' teaching
"unless you become like a child
you cannot enter the kingdom of heaven."

The preceding clarifications represent Logic Smart.

We preachers sometimes
quote that verse
and then deliver a sermon
that only an adult could understand.
We talk about the verse
but we don't enact it in our preaching.

Today I want to become
childlike
in my sermon,
and consider the feeding of the five thousand
from the perspective
of Isaiah,
the little boy with five barley loaves
and two fish.

I am going to preach
in a more childlike way,
and I invite you to listen
in a more childlike way
because
as Jesus taught,
"Unless you become like a child
you cannot enter the kingdom of heaven."

The preacher demonstrates Self Smart.

"Isaiah. Isaaaaaiah!
You didn't eat the lunch
I packed for you."

"Yes, I did, Mom.
Honest.
I ate the whole thing."

Music Smart: the preacher uses again the same vocal inflection that started the sermon to indicate we have now moved out of the logical adult explanations and returned to the story line.

"No. You didn't.
I'm looking at it.
It's right in front of me.
I know what I'm seeing.
It's all right here,
two fish: one, two...three...
Four?!
Five barley loaves: one, two three, four, five...six...
Seven?!

(Even the mother depicts Literal Larry's way of knowing: truth is
what can be proved concretely.)
Logic Smart.

"Isaiah:
What's going on here?
Is this the same basket
I gave you this morning?
Did you bring home
somebody else's lunch?"

"No, Mom.
Look, its got the bent handle."

(He refers to a visible and tangible reality.)

"Yeah, you're right.
One, two, three, four.
Four fish.
One, two, three, four, five, six, seven.
Seven barley loaves.

"Isaiah,
let me get this straight.
You left home
with two fish and five barley loaves.
Is that right or not?"

"Yep, Mom, that's right."

"You ate your lunch
and then you brought
home more than
when you left.

Is that right or not?"

"Well.
Not exactly.
You see:
first I gave my lunch away,
then I ate my lunch,
then I brought home more than when I left."

(The exchange stays on the level of the concrete. Note also the linear narrative form of the child's response that is characteristic of Literal Larry's way of knowing.)

"Isaiah.
Talk sense.
You're gonna drive me crazy.
You can't give something away,
then eat it,
and then have more than when you gave it away in the first place.
That's impossible.
Things don't work that way."

(Here the mother uses concrete reasoning to question the child's claim of concrete truth.)

"But things do work that way."

"What do you mean,
'they work that way'?
Explain it to me."

"Well . . .
I don't know that I can explain it.
All I can do is
tell you what happened."

(The child stays on the concrete narrative level and cannot provide hypothetical reasons for what he literally experienced.)

"Okay.
What happened?"

"I went out to hear
that man.
You know.
The guy who's good with stories.
He always likes it when kids show up.
Some of the adults
are always telling us to leave.
But he always says,
'Let 'em stay.
Let 'em come right up front if they want.'
So I went up the hill
where he was seated.
All his best buddies
are kinda in a circle around him.
I put the picnic basket
right next to me."

(This can represent Magical Maggie's view of persons as big or little and a bunch of individuals with a boss, and/or Literal Larry's view of a group of individuals with some sense of two-way usefulness—Jesus and his buddies.)

This portrayal of the scene is Picture Smart and Body Smart.

"Then he starts telling his stories.
That's what I went to hear."

"What are the stories about?"

"About sheep and seeds,
about somebody who gets mugged
and is lying in the road,
about some kid
who asks for all the allowance ever owed him,
and he gets it!
Then he runs away from home,
ends up eating pig slop,
comes back home,
and they throw him a big party.
You know,
that kind of thing."

(The one-dimensional narrative focus of Literal Larry.)
Some use of Nature Smart.

"What's the point of the stories?"

"The point?"

"I mean:
what do the stories mean?"

(The mother wants to know some abstract meaning characteristic of
an adult way of knowing.)

"I don't know.
I'm still figuring that out.
They're just good stories.
They keep going on in my head.
They're doing something to me."

(The child stays on the level of concrete narrative.)

"All right. All right.
So you're sitting up close to him on the hill.
His friends are there.
The picnic basket is next to you.
And you're listening to the stories.
What happens next?"

Visualizing the scene is Picture Smart.

"A lot more people
start coming."

"What do you mean a lot?
Ten, fifteen, twenty?"

"Oh no, Mom,
I mean a lot more."

"What's a lot more?"

"Millions of them!"

(It is still concrete, but appears like fantasy thinking characteristic of
Magical Maggie.)

"It couldn't have been millions of them.
Talk sense, Isaiah."

"Okay, maybe it wasn't millions.
But everywhere I looked there were people.
Everywhere.
I mean all over."

"So there is a crowd of people
plus the teacher's friends

and you're sitting up close
with your picnic basket.
What happened next?"

"After a lot of stories,
you can see people are getting hungry.
You know how people look
when they need something to eat.
So the teacher asks his friends,
'Where are we going to get some bread
for these people?'

"His friends look over the hill,
and they tell him,
there's no way it's gonna happen
'cause it would take
globs and globs of money to feed all those people.

(Even the disciples think of truth here in terms of what can be proved
concretely!)
Logic Smart.

"Then this one friend of his
points to me, and says,
'Here's a kid with a picnic basket.'
His friend looks down in it and counts,
'One, two'—two fish.
One, two, three, four, five—five barley loaves.
That's all he's got.'

**The counting again uses Logic Smart, and Body Smart as the
preacher uses fingers to count.**

"I throw my arms around the basket
and hug it close.
I'm not going to give up my lunch
just because a million adults
were too stupid to bring their own."

(Typical of Literal Larry's way of knowing: what is right is "what I
want!")

"Then the teacher looks at me.
I can tell he's not going to force me
to give up my lunch."

"How can you tell that, Isaiah?"

"Oh, I don't know.
Maybe because of the tone of his voice
when he tells his stories.
Maybe because when I looked in his face,
he made me think of you, Mom."

(Authority for Literal Larry's perspective is located in persons who
earn recognition for their abilities. In this case the child grants such
authority to his mother and to Jesus.)

"What did you do then?"

"I gave him the basket."

"You gave him the basket?
The whole thing?
I packed that lunch for you.
You didn't take anything out for yourself?
At least a loaf
or one of the fish?"

"Nope.
I gave him the whole thing."

"Why did you do that?"

"I don't know.
I just gave it to him.
His voice, his stories, his face.
I like that man, Mom.
He's very kind.
You'd like him too, Mom.
I bet you would do the same thing.
You would give him your lunch,
if you saw and heard him."

(Again the child thinks about authority from the perspective of
Literal Larry.)
In naming what he likes the child shows that he is Self Smart.

"What did he do with it?"

"He put his hands
on the basket with the bread and the fish,
and he prayed.
Then he got up
and starts passing the basket to the people.
He comes to me, and says,
'Take what you need.'
So I took two fish and five barley loaves,
and he moved on to the next person,
and soon you can hear
people all over the hill
passing the basket to one another,
and saying 'Take what you need.'
Take what you need.

Take what you need.
Take what you need.
Take what you need …

(The child's concrete narrative also embodies Literal Larry's notion of fairness in the invitation to "take what you need.")
The rhythmic "take what you need" is repeated more and more softly to suggest the voices going out to the far edges of the crowd. The preacher's voice thus blends Picture Smart and Music Smart.

"When it's all over,
his buddies gather what's left
and they have enough to fill twelve baskets.

"He puts four fish and seven loaves
in my basket
because that's all it will hold
and hands it back to me.
Honest, Mom, that's all I can tell you."

"But how do you explain it, Isaiah?
How did it happen?"

(The mother again wants a more hypothetical response, but receives the child's concrete narrative of what he was enjoying.)

"I don't know.
I wasn't worrying about explanations
while I was eating.
I was just enjoying the fish
and the barley loaves,
and I was thanking God
I still had my lunch to eat after giving it away.
Then I realized it was time to leave

so I started home.
It's a long walk
from the hill next to the lake
back to here.
But I didn't mind.
All the way home
I kept thinking about his stories
and about what had happened."

The child's reflection is Self Smart, and his description is Nature Smart.

"What were you thinking, Isaiah?"

"Oh, I just was thinking
you can feed a whole lot more people
than you ever thought you could.
What you gotta do
is give what you got
to this guy Jesus.
Doesn't matter how little you got.
Have Jesus pray over it.
And there will be enough,
enough for everyone.

(Note that the child narrates what happened without making an abstract claim or an adult explanation. By staying in concrete operations, the sermon leaves it to adult listeners to bring their own ways of knowing to the story.)

"Here, Mom, take what you need."
(The preacher stretches out an arm toward the congregation as though offering them a basket with fish and bread. The sermon thus concludes with the child continuing in concrete operations.)
The closing gesture is Body Smart and Picture Smart.

FIVE BENEFITS OF USING CHILDREN'S WAYS OF KNOWING IN A SERMON

1. Children's ways of knowing can help a preacher create parabolic sermons that engage adult ways of thinking. Childlike parabolic preaching is not anti-intellectual nor does it involve speaking down to people. It is rather an invitation to another perception of reality, a perception that we once had as children and that is still accessible to us. Sadly, we too often ignore it, to the impoverishment of the life of faith and the vitality of our imaginations.

After delivering the sermon I was delighted with the number of people who told me that the child's telling of the story helped them see the familiar passage as if again for the first time, and it "got them to thinking …" In this respect the sermon carried on the ancient tradition of *midrashim*, elaborations upon sacred Scripture that the rabbis provided "for the sake of maintaining the continued vitality of the text."[15] Telling the well-known story from the child's point of view awakened a lot of vitality in the congregation. The spectrum of adult thinking ranged from issues of personal growth to social justice. One person said that she frequently prayed for others but never for herself because she feared it was being too selfish. But in the sermon she heard Christ saying to her that she ought to pray for herself as well as others: "Take what *you* need." Another listener came away thinking that there are enough resources in the world for everyone if we only will heed the instruction, "Take what you *need*, not what you *want*." And these are only two of the responses that I heard.

I preached the sermon a second time in a church that had about sixty young children in attendance. I preached it as a sermon for the whole congregation. That evening I saw the mother of one of the children, who reported to me that her child had retold the sermon in her presence to a friend when they stopped on the way home to pick up some milk. She was astounded because the child remembered the whole thing. This was possible because the sermon engaged the child's ways of knowing.

The parabolic character of the sermon arises from its concreteness, a quality shared by Jesus' own storytelling. Preaching in this mode is a way of following Christ, who trusted that his parabolic preaching, living, and being would lead us into a deeper relationship with God. Where God reigns there is no longer any need to be anxious whether or not the congregation got the point. The listeners do much better than getting the point. They start doing exactly what Lowry says: they make connections to their life and ministry that the preacher never could have anticipated. They open their hearts and minds to the Spirit whose movement none of us controls.

2. *Children's ways of knowing allow room for different ways of interpreting the Bible.* In the same congregation I have found adults who believe the miracle of the loaves and fishes occurred exactly as described in the Bible while others take the story to be symbolic of what happens when Christ empowers us to share generously what we have. Arguing in a sermon for only one of these interpretations (or any number of other possibilities) is counterproductive. The preacher will seldom, if ever, change anyone's mind. But staying in concrete operations allows room for these different interpretations while at the same time getting to the child's crucial insight that with Christ's blessing we can feed a lot more people than we think we can. Instead of arguing about whose biblical interpretation is right, we can use our energy to feed the hungry.

3. *Children's ways of knowing are a gift to the whole community of God, children and adults alike.* By treating seriously a child's perception and idiom we avoid speaking down to children in the patronizing tone that is sometimes the affliction of children's sermons. When the whole community of faith learns from children, it demonstrates greater respect for their being fully members of the Body of Christ. But it does something else as well: it honors adults by assuming that they have the capacity to become like children in order to enter the reign of God.

It is not realistic nor helpful to preach every sermon using primarily children's ways of knowing. But there is no reason at all that you cannot employ such ways of knowing regularly in your preaching. As Carolyn Brown astutely observes: "Many sermons or points within a sermon are directed to specific groups within the congregation. The rest of the congregation is invited to listen in and to make application to their own situations. I ask not that every sermon be focused on children, but that you preach with as much awareness of the children as of their elders."[16]

4. *Using children's ways of knowing in sermons gives witness that God is concerned for the whole story of our lives.* All adults bring with them a trail of memories from their childhood, and a great deal of working out our "own salvation with fear and trembling" (Philippians 2:12) involves bringing those memories to God, the memories of joy and gratitude, the memories of hurt and sorrow, the memories that have empowered us to be our best selves, and the memories that have wounded us. The process of memory and coming to terms with the past continues throughout our lives. If we live a long life and our short-term memory begins to fade, the childhood memories often stay with us. In light of the life cycle, it is important that the preaching of the church not make the gospel sound as though it is reserved for adult understanding alone. Our homiletic needs to give witness to how God's love reaches to us in every generation, and using children's ways of knowing as well as adult ways of knowing in our sermons is a major way of providing pastoral care to every age of listener.

5. *Children's ways of knowing foster the rebirth of wonder.* We opened this chapter with the story of little Susan who wanted to stop by the church and feed the baby Jesus after the Christmas pageant. We adults often say "Christmas is for children" because the children are the ones who most help us see the astonishment and wonder of the incarnation. There are three big adult words in that last sentence: "astonishment," "wonder," "incarnation." As adults, we can use them in a sentence that makes reasonable sense. But it is the little girl pointing out that someone needs to feed the baby Jesus who gives us access to the affective dimensions of our adult concepts.

There is no need to limit the rebirth of wonder to once a year at Christmas. Using children's ways of knowing in our sermons throughout the year can renew again and again our astonishment at who God is and who God made us to be. That is a gift of the Spirit too precious for any preacher or church to ignore.

CHAPTER 4

PREACHING AND ADULT WAYS OF KNOWING

IT DEPENDS ON YOUR PERSPECTIVE

I (Tom) can still see in my mind's eye the high hill that rose above the northern shore of the lake where I grew up. Our town was at the southern end, seven miles away. When you looked north, the hill appeared to be the profile of a sleeping lion comfortably stretched out on its stomach. Its back rose gradually up from the east, until it curved more steeply to the summit that formed the mane and the head. Then the western most slope became more gradual, as if it were the outstretched paws. The locals called the high hill Sleeping Lion. When the aurora borealis unfurled in the wintry skies, people would ask the next day, "Did you see the northern lights playing over Sleeping Lion?"

If, however, you drove along the west lake road or boated north and looked at Sleeping Lion head-on from where its "paws" touched the shore, the hill looked like a scoop of ice cream. But the hill never got named Scoop of Ice Cream. Nobody ever asked, "Did you see the northern lights playing over Scoop of Ice Cream?" Few people lived at the northern end of the lake, and the dominant perspective was from the town where the hill indeed appeared to be a sleeping lion.

It depends on your perspective.

But that is not just true of objects. It is also true of events. Consider the phenomenon of instant replay at sporting events. Sometimes, for example, in a football game there will be a dispute whether a player stepped out of bounds or not. Officials and fans look at the play over and over from different angles. In one stop-action shot the player appears to be in bounds, but in another the toe of his boot appears to be ever so slightly over the line. It depends on your perspective.

In the case of the game, there is a complicating twist to our perspective. If the player is on the team we are rooting for, then we will say, "No, he's not out. Look, his toe is just inside. It's close, but he's in bounds." On the other hand, if we are rooting for the opposing side and the penalty means our team will now get the ball, we will say, "He is out of bounds. You can see the toe is just over the line." It all depends on your perspective. But in the case of the game, the concept of perspective is much more complicated. It includes the physical perspective, the angle from which the shot was taken, but it also includes what the fans bring to the act of viewing the replay: their emotional investment in the game and the hopes they have riding on their team.

You can go to my hometown and view Sleeping Lion, then drive north and see Scoop of Ice Cream, and although you will perhaps call it something else, the difference the perspective makes will be easy to detect. But a human event in which people are emotionally invested and to which they bring their values, their hopes, and their particular ways of knowing makes for a more nuanced and complex understanding of what constitutes a perspective.

THE CHURCH AS A COGNITIVELY INCLUSIVE COMMUNITY

Like the fans at the game, congregation members bring particular perspectives to receiving, processing, and responding to sermons. As David Buttrick puts the matter: "Perspective is much more than angles of perception. Point-of-view can be *attitudinal.* We are seldom dispassionate people."[1] We find that cognitive theories confirm and expand Buttrick's insight. It shows us that our varied perspectives represent different patterns of knowing, patterns that manifest themselves in how preachers create sermons and how listeners respond to them. As we saw in chapter 2, different listeners create different sermons from the sermon the preacher delivers. So far we have traced how the theories of Multiple Intelligences and children's ways of knowing can help us understand and enrich the interaction between preacher and congregation. In this chapter, we offer a theory of four adult ways of knowing—four perspectives—that can expand your ability to reach a greater variety of listeners.

As we did with children's ways of knowing, we personify these four adult ways to help you keep in mind each one's unique and distinguishing characteristics.

Affiliating Al
Bargaining Betty
Conceptualizing Charles
Dialectical Donna

Like Magical Maggie and Literal Larry in chapter 3, the names do not represent actual individuals. We do not use the typology to label people. The alliterative names are heuristic devices to help you remember the different perspectives.[2] Some of the experienced preachers who have taken our course playfully recall the names as they review their sermons. It helps them detect which perspectives they have featured and which they have neglected. It aids them in figuring out how to preach the gospel from multiple perspectives so that they engage all of us for all of God. The alliterative names are a reminder that every time we speak "we will be speaking some particular point-of-view, whether we are aware of it or not. *Perspectival language forms the consciousness of a congregation*; it shapes congregational point-of-view. By our speaking we form angles in congregational consciousness, perspectives, depths, attitudes.... Point-of-view is not an occasional rhetorical device, it *is* speaking. The language of preaching, as all human language, is radically perspectival."[3] The study of adult ways of knowing sharpens our capacity to form "angles in congregational consciousness" by reminding us of the multiple perspectives in the congregation that work to form what Reuel Howe called "the church's sermon."

Although he does not use Howe's terms, David Buttrick helps us understand how the preacher sets in motion the church's sermon: "Preaching is language aimed at communal consciousness, the consciousness of a congregation."[4] Buttrick points out that this involves more than preaching to the personal needs of individual listeners: "While it may be helpful to bring to mind particular people in situations during the preparation of sermons, actually the language of preaching is shaped for *common* consciousness."[5]

We have discovered that preachers cannot take "common consciousness" for granted. Even if "we share a 'cultural formulation' shaped by common language and common myths, symbols and idioms,"[6] maintaining congregational consciousness still requires attention to the multiple ways of adult knowing in the congregation. Preachers nurture the congregational consciousness by employing different adult perspectives, by honoring their unique contributions, and by modeling in their sermons how the different perspectives can work together. Preachers thus make the church a cognitively inclusive community where one way of knowing does not dominate all the others.

Although preaching is our focus, developing a congregational *ethos* that honors multiple perspectives also depends on how we act in other areas of church life. One day in class we simulated a church board meeting, randomly assigning one of the four perspectives to each experienced pastor. The board was asked to make a decision about a controversial issue. The pastors kept their real names in the simulation, but they shaped their remarks in light of their randomly assigned perspectives: Affiliating Al, Bargaining Betty, Conceptualizing Charles, or Dialectical Donna.

When we debriefed after the simulation, some students said it was effortless to use the perspective they had been given because they used it all the time in real life. But others found they had to work hard at thinking from the perspective assigned them because it was inimical to their usual way of looking at things. Trying out a new perspective in the simulation gave the pastors insight about people whose ways of thinking had often baffled them.

The class of experienced pastors simulating the board meeting did not easily reach agreement on the controversial topic. Honoring the different cognitive perspectives is not a recipe for erasing the genuine disagreement that exists between people about matters of substance. But the pastors discovered that being attentive to different ways of adult knowing is a practical method for creating new strategies to engage the whole congregation. The pastors began to have a more accurate map of the congregational *ethos*. Their preaching could more effectively feed the sermon that everyone has a part in creating, the sermon that Howe calls "the church's sermon."

In the sections that follow we give examples not only from preaching but also from many other areas of church life: hymns, social issues, worship space, church meetings, symbols, matters of justice and law. We include this wide range of matters because preachers can learn about the different ways of knowing present in a congregation by listening carefully to how people talk about these things. It is a way for preachers "to bring their pre-sermonic reflection into the largest possible conversation."[7]

THINKING ABOUT THINKING

In the interviews with the young boy reported in chapter 3, we observed that the acquisition of abstract thinking by age twelve was a key structural change in the child's ways of knowing. Abstract thinking can be defined as "thinking about thinking" or "coming up with ideas that are generated from what we experience as tangible and literal." When the boy was six he thought that the parable of the lost sheep and the ninety-nine would give people "stupid ideas." But at age twelve he drew from the parable a general principle, saying Jesus told the story "to explain to people that there may be a hundred people but if one dies you might say, 'Well, one out of a hundred really doesn't matter,' but one out of a hundred really does matter." His ways of knowing had developed to the point that he was capable of formulating an insight based on the story. The capacity for abstract thinking was emerging in the child's thought processes.

Most adults are capable of abstract thinking, but abstract thinking is not monolithic. It does not follow a single uniform pattern. As John McClure has observed: "Every homiletic model for reason presupposes an epistemology [a way of knowing]. Underlying our assertions or claims in preaching that something is true, and the way that we make those claims, is a process for understanding how we can know anything at all about the world in which we live."[8] We will consider four distinct epistemologies, four ways of knowing or perspectives that characterize the abstract thinking of different adults as represented by our alliterative names: Affiliating Al, Bargaining Betty, Conceptualizing Charles, and Dialectical Donna. Each is unique. Each is valuable in its own right. Each can profit from being in relationship with the others.

Since thinking about thinking is strenuous work, we have organized the rest of this chapter to allow for the different ways of adult knowing that readers bring to this book. Here is an overview of the material, and then some suggestions about how you might approach it.

First, we describe and give examples of six characteristics of each adult way of knowing:

1. View of the World (examples: favorite hymns)

2. Reasoning (examples: perspectives on a hot issue)

3. Symbols (examples: responses to rebuilding the chancel)

4. Community/Society (examples: contributions to a church mission statement)

5. Justice (examples: decisions about punishing a wrongdoer)

6. Biblical Interpretation (examples: favorite Bible passages)

Next, we offer a chart that summarizes these characteristics. Finally, we share three sermons that illustrate the theory in practice.

Some readers may want to move sequentially through the material, from the list of characteristics and examples to the summarizing chart to the sermons. Others, however, may want to proceed more inductively, first perusing the sermons and then referring to the list of characteristics and the summarizing chart. Still others may want to flip back and forth between the sermons and the chart.

One final hint about grasping these different perspectives: you might try what the experienced pastors did when they simulated a church meeting on a controversial topic. Identify an issue that is alive in your church or a text or a topic that you need to address in a sermon. Then systematically try thinking about it from each perspective. When is it easiest to do this? When is it more difficult? We assume that the readers of this book will themselves manifest different ways of knowing and learning!

SIX CHARACTERISTICS OF EACH ADULT WAY OF KNOWING

1. View of World

Affiliating Al views the world primarily in terms of interpersonal relationships and the values of significant persons whom he seeks to emulate.

Bargaining Betty, although she knows the world is filled with a vast diversity of views, bets that her preferences are the best. However, she will not impose her views on others who believe differently as long as they do not impose their views on her. That is "the bargain" she strikes with them.

Conceptualizing Charles views the world through reason. He is interested in his own and other people's concepts and ideologies. Being rational is vitally important.

Dialectical Donna sees the world as ambiguous, complex, and in some cases paradoxical. She is concerned with developing her own integrative vision of the world and her place in it.

Examples

If you asked congregation members to name a favorite hymn and explain why they chose it, here are ways that the different perspectives might manifest themselves.

Affiliating Al: "What a Friend We Have in Jesus" because of the strong interpersonal connection to the savior and the deep feelings of warmth awakened by both the words and the musical setting.

Bargaining Betty: "In Christ There Is No East or West" because it celebrates a great diversity of people who are not forcing themselves on one another but rather are bound in "one great fellowship of love."

Conceptualizing Charles: "God, Who Stretched the Spangled Heavens" because it acknowledges the validity of our scientific discoveries and calls us to think rationally about their implications. We have traveled through "realms of space;/Probed the secrets of the atom,/Yielding unimagined power,/Facing us with life's destruction/Or our most triumphant hour."

Dialectical Donna: "Immortal, Invisible God Only Wise" because she likes the complexity and paradox that the poetry offers: "In light inaccessible hid from our eyes." "In all life thou livest the true life of all."

2. Reasoning

Affiliating Al is able to think abstractly. He constructs hypotheses about his experiences, but his thinking is compartmentalized: for example, he cannot provide a rational analysis of why he values Christian love but hates certain groups. His reasoning is embedded in his feelings, making it difficult to separate one from the other. His idea of truth comes with a strong emotional conviction that it is absolute and right.

96

Bargaining Betty also constructs abstract hypotheses about her life experiences, and she invests those constructions with strong feelings. She is aware of differences of opinion and tries to analyze and evaluate those differences. Her essential criterion, however, is not logic but what she feels. She generalizes her way of thinking to others: whatever they feel is true is acceptable, providing they do not impose it on someone else who feels differently.

Conceptualizing Charles analyzes everything. He trusts rationality based on clear criteria, consistency, and coherence. Charles is more concerned with the validity of ideas than with some absolute and abstract notion of truth. Once he is convinced that he has constructed a valid argument, he holds to it with passion. He will often draw a sharp dichotomy between his understanding and those with whom he disagrees.

Dialectical Donna holds in tension ambiguities and paradoxes as she seeks to integrate differences and opposites into her own vision of truth. She analyzes various systems of thought including that to which she is committed, and evaluates them from a critically self-aware perspective. For her all claims of truth can be examined critically, especially in terms of how they have developed communally throughout history.

Examples

Let us imagine that you are at a church board meeting to discuss a controversial issue: should the board support the pastor's development and use of a rite to celebrate nonmarital relationships, including same-sex unions? Why or why not? Here are ways the different patterns of reasoning might manifest themselves. For each perspective we show both an affirmative and negative position because different individuals using the same pattern of reasoning may come to different conclusions.[9]

Affiliating Al might conclude yes, because nonmarried elderly and same-sex couples are faithful, dedicated, and loving to each other. The church should develop rules and rites to celebrate that kind of good behavior.

OR

Affiliating Al might conclude no, because the Bible and "our" tradition absolutely limit liturgical rites to heterosexual married couples. It is just not right.

Bargaining Betty might conclude yes, because that is what the pastor wants to do. Also, she does not like the idea that some people who do not agree are trying to impose their views on the pastor and upon others who feel it is perfectly all right to have these rites.

OR

Bargaining Betty might conclude no, because the pastor will want to make that rite into a rule for others who do not feel it is right. Imposing on others like that is not a loving thing to do.

Conceptualizing Charles might conclude yes, even though the national denomination did not vote to approve the creation of these liturgical rites, there is a valid rationale for creating these liturgical rites. They can be defended in light of Jesus' understanding of family as those who hear God's word and do it. Contemporary experience has led many to redefine the meaning of family in our society.

OR

Conceptualizing Charles might conclude no, because the pastor must obey the existing polity of the church. Church polity is established to structure and maintain the institutional church for its ministry. We are free to work to change the denomination's policy, but for now it still stands.

Dialectical Donna might conclude yes, because the denomination did affirm the equal worth of all persons. That is a universal principle to be embodied in church law, and it is the standard by which church law is to be evaluated. She honors the minister's commitment to that principle by creating a liturgical rite to celebrate the equal worth and dignity of each person and each committed relationship. Also, we need to view the proposal in light of the fact that there has been liturgical innovation throughout the history of the church.

OR

Dialectical Donna might conclude no, because, although respecting the appeal to the universal principle of the equal worth of all persons, the pastor's decision of conscience would subvert the current church polity, which is understood as a social contract created through the due process of communal thought and action.

3. Symbols

Affiliating Al has profound affective connections to those symbols important to his life experience. The symbol and the reality symbolized are inseparably bound together. Tampering with the symbol feels like tampering with the reality. God is personal with human qualities like a friend or a father who cares and protects. God may also be understood as a judge who punishes or forgives.

Bargaining Betty is aware that a symbol may have multiple abstract meanings to which it is bound. She settles questions about different interpretations of a symbol on the basis of her feelings and preferences. While she feels that God is personal and has human qualities, she is open to others feeling differently from herself. But she does not want anyone to mess around with the symbols to which she has a strong emotive connection.

Conceptualizing Charles might be tempted to confront the perspectives of Affiliating Al and Bargaining Betty because for him a symbol is just a symbol. It can be rationally separated from the conceptual reality to which it refers. God may be personal for Charles, but is often conceived in more abstract terms such as justice, human liberation, Creator, force, or ground of being.

Dialectical Donna thinks that symbols both point to and participate in the reality they symbolize. She understands that symbols are partial and relative but that they also have generative power to create new possibilities for individuals and communities. For Donna the divine is complex and paradoxical. God is personal and abstract, God is near and far.

Examples

Imagine a chancel whose most striking feature is a stained glass window that pictures Jesus as the good shepherd carrying a sheep. The church is getting ready to refurbish the chancel. Because there is a lot of heat loss through the window in the winter, one of the suggested plans calls for its removal, filling in the hole, and hanging a backlit cross. Here is how the different ways of relating to symbols might manifest themselves.

Affiliating Al protests the plan as strongly as possible. Every Sunday he looks at that window and feels Jesus carrying him through life. To take out the window would rob him of this close interpersonal relationship to the good shepherd.

Bargaining Betty has the same feelings about the window as Affiliating Al, and she resents that others want to impose their new design upon them.

Conceptualizing Charles is utterly impatient with both of them. Why can they not see that it is just a window? A building consultant has pointed out there is extreme heat loss through the window, and with fuel prices skyrocketing, it makes perfect sense to replace the window with a solid wall. Furthermore, the cross is the central symbol of the faith, and the backlit cross will point to the same savior that the window does now.

Dialectical Donna has researched in the church archives the many chancel changes that have taken place since the church was built. She points out the window was not there until several decades ago, the last time the chancel was redesigned. Like Charles she sees that the cross and the good shepherd both point to Christ, but she is also concerned for Al and Betty and how Christ lives within them. She suggests that they could mount the window inside the parish hall where it would be prominently displayed and protected from the elements. Then they could proceed with the remodeling of the chancel.

4. Community/Society

Affiliating Al identifies with people who share his values, feelings, and opinions, but his circle does not include others who are different. Al values people who live good, loving lives according to the standards of his community. Law provides the guidelines for good behavior and preventing chaos.

Bargaining Betty also connects with people who share her feelings, values, and opinions, but she is aware that there are multiple opportunities for being in community. She will sort out differences among various communal groups according to her own preferences, and tolerate groups other than her own as long as they are not coercive. She understands that law protects an individual's right to have personal preferences and feelings.

Conceptualizing Charles thinks about community in terms of the structures that hold it together. He will investigate a community's infrastructure of rules, laws, procedures, and sanctions to determine if it is viable and capable of maintaining itself. Law protects legal rights and maintains the stability of society and its institutions. He honors people who live according to a system's values and contribute to the community.

Dialectical Donna values a community that is open and inclusive and that provides for the participation of all people through commonly held agreements and processes. Laws and rules are honored as long as they embody and enhance the intrinsic value of every person. Donna seeks to create a society in which all persons are treated equally.

Examples

The ruling board of a church has decided it is time to rewrite the congregation's mission statement. They are eager to formulate a fresh vision of the church's ministry. The board members have put in the worship bulletin a description of their work and ask that everyone finish the following sentence: "We as a church are committed to . . ." Here are some ways the various perspectives on community/society might be reflected in the finished sentences people submit.

Affiliating Al: "We as a church are committed to being a community where you can feel the warmth of Christian fellowship."

Bargaining Betty: "We as a church are committed to respecting each person's way of believing."

Conceptualizing Charles: "We as a church are committed to doing things decently and in order."

Dialectical Donna: "We as a church are committed to living faithfully in a pluralistic world of multiple cultural and religious perspectives."

5. Justice

Affiliating Al defines justice according to conventional images of good behavior. People are just if they conform to these conventions and unjust if they do not. It is important to live your good intentions.

Bargaining Betty defines justice in much the same way as Al. However, being aware of varying definitions of conventional behavior, Betty will not condemn persons who do not conform, providing they have good intentions and do not impose their behavior on others.

Conceptualizing Charles believes that the just person is a responsible contributor to the well-being of society. Those who violate or destroy the social system, be it church or state, are unjust and should be punished.

Dialectical Donna understands that legal systems are essential to the establishment of justice. But she also sees how systems can work for good and for ill, sometimes protecting the equal worth of all persons and sometimes abrogating that essential principle. Therefore, in pursuing justice her thinking moves back and forth between legal systems and moral values so that they check and balance each other.

Examples

Imagine that a longtime member of the church, who has served honorably for many years as the church treasurer, is now discovered using church funds to sustain an addiction he developed after his beloved wife died tragically. The ruling board is meeting to discuss what they should do. Here are some ways the various perspectives might shape people's responses. As in the case of the contested social issue, we give two possibilities for each perspective since our focus is on the pattern of knowing rather than the conclusion that is reached.

Affiliating Al has had a long friendship with the treasurer and feels that the man needs our help, not our condemnation, especially in light of the tragic circumstances.

OR

Affiliating Al says the law is the law. What the man did is unjust. The church and society will fall to pieces if such behavior is not punished.

Bargaining Betty feels we have to remember all the years the treasurer served honorably, and now as long as the money can be returned over time, she does not believe we should impose a severe punishment on one who has already endured enough tragedy.

OR

Bargaining Betty resents how the treasurer's misuse of funds has forced the church into a tight fiscal situation as well as disrupted its ministry, thus imposing the consequences of his addiction on the whole group. The board must take legal action to protect the congregation.

Conceptualizing Charles has read about grief reactions and addictive behaviors, and it has helped him to analyze and understand the psychological dynamics behind this sad story. Therefore, it is valid for mercy to temper justice in this case.

OR

Conceptualizing Charles, while understanding the causes, still believes that individuals must be responsible to the organizations in which they work. We have devised a system of law to protect our institutions, and if we fail to use it in a situation like this we invite disaster.

Dialectical Donna suggests the board should hold in tension three distinct but interrelated aspects to the case: the pastoral care of the treasurer whose life has fallen apart, the need to act in a way that will restore the confidence of the congregation in the oversight of its funds, and the requirements of the law.

OR

Dialectical Donna decides that while the board should provide pastoral support for the treasurer, the sense of betrayal and hurt in the congregation is so great that they must act as swiftly and prudently as possible. First, the board should meet with a lawyer and a denominational consultant, then, in light of their professional counsel, formulate and carry out a plan.

6. Biblical Interpretation

Affiliating Al looks for the basic meaning in a biblical text that he can use as a guideline and example to follow. He wants to know the true meaning of a text and how it can be useful. Al is not interested in extensive analysis or exegesis of any text. But he likes stories and images to which he can relate at a strong feeling level.

Bargaining Betty also interprets biblical texts to discover the messages and guidelines that are useful for her. She is aware the Bible has different meanings for different people. What is good for her may not be good for others, and vice versa. In her search for meaning in the Bible she finds extensive analysis to be boring and distracting.

Conceptualizing Charles can be passionate about the concepts, images, themes, meanings, and doctrines he is able to abstract from a biblical text through rigorous literary and historical criticism. He may also be fascinated by the critical study of the Bible in and of itself. Charles will seek to establish rational and coherent conclusions through his analysis of a given set of texts. He asks if an interpretation is valid.

Dialectical Donna interprets the Bible as a dialogue partner, as a subject and not just an object to scrutinize. She analyzes texts to discover their abstract meanings and integrate them into her own self-understanding. Her study of the Bible becomes a personal confrontation with the ultimate reality to which the Bible points from within the context of its various communities and traditions. She wants to know how to integrate new meanings with her personal commitment.

Examples

Imagine a preacher who is thinking of a sermon series on beloved biblical texts. The preacher asks congregation members to e-mail their favorite text. The various adult ways of knowing might emerge in choices like these:

Affiliating Al chooses Matthew 11:28-30: "Come to me, all you that are weary and are carrying heavy burdens, and I will give you rest. Take my yoke upon you, and learn from me; for I am gentle and humble in heart, and you will find rest for your souls. For my yoke is easy, and my burden is light." This is the compassionate Jesus who loves Al and whom Al loves in return.

Bargaining Betty chooses from the Sermon on the Mount, the Golden Rule, Matthew 7:12: "In everything do to others as you would have them do to you; for this is the law and prophets." If everyone lived this way, they would respect those who differ from them and not impose their ideas and practices on others.

Conceptualizing Charles chooses Exodus 20:3-17, the Ten Commandments, because they are a clear, reasonable foundation for a well-ordered and just society.

Dialectical Donna chooses Luke's version of a sermon by Paul in Athens in Luke 17:22-31 because it defines God as the one in whom "we live and move and have our being" (Acts 17:28). She is committed to this integrative vision of God because it suggests how even our fragmented and paradoxical human existence is contained in a larger divine reality.

A Summary Chart of Different Ways of Adult Knowing

The following chart summarizes the distinctive features of the four ways of adult knowing.

AFFILIATING AL	BARGAINING BETTY
Interpersonal	Interpersonal relationships
Not analytical	Analysis not separated from feelings
Feelings	
Absolutes	Whatever anyone feels is true
Symbol & reality inseparably bound	Tolerance of others who are not coercive
Symbols have one true meaning	Symbols have multiple meanings
Feelings bound with symbol	Symbol & reality inseparably bound
God as personal	
Affectional groups	Preferences bound with symbol
Persons loved & good	God with personal qualities
Law prevents chaos	Multiple affectional groups
Justice: good intentions	Persons are more important
Bible: true meanings	Law protects preferences
	Justice: good intentions & not coercive
	Bible: Different meanings for different people

CONCEPTUALIZING CHARLES	DIALECTICAL DONNA
Centered on rational systems	Pluralistic & ambiguous
Consistency & coherence	Dialectical/paradoxical
Valid versus true	Integration & commitment
Symbol separated from conceptual reality	Symbol participates in reality
Rational bonding to symbol's concept	Emotional/rational bonding to new vision
God concepts: justice, power	God in all God's complexity
Social & institutional structures	Open and inclusive society
Persons contribute to systems	Intrinsic value of persons
Law structures and maintains society	Law preserves basic rights
Justice: maintain social systems	Justice: universal principles; legal/moral
Bible: abstract concepts and meanings	Bible: dialogue partner with others

PUTTING THE THEORY TO PRACTICE WHEN WE PREACH

There is no magical formula for applying this theory of adult ways of knowing to the preparation and evaluation of sermons. Persons who preach regularly already know about these differences through their experience and intuition. The theory, however, provides a structure for guiding those intuitive understandings so that preaching for adult ways of knowing can be more intentional and effective. Through practice, anyone can refine the art. This will undoubtedly involve experimenting with various forms of sermons and avoiding getting locked into only one way of preaching.

The experienced preachers in our course have used the chart to create and analyze sermons by one another, as well as sermons that they preached in their congregations. They discovered that some perspectives were harder for them to embody than others because of their own natural predilections. But it was worth the effort because their expanding repertoire of cognitive strategies reached more of the congregation. It helped them engage all of us for all of God.

We now share three sermons that put the theory to homiletical use. Before you read through them, we encourage you to place a bookmark at the summary chart or make a photocopy so that you can refer to it as you analyze how the preacher is employing a particular adult way of knowing. If using the chart alone you are unable to identify how the sermon employs the theory, you may want to go back to the fuller prose descriptions and examples of each adult way of knowing.

The first sermon uses primarily the perspective of Affiliating Al. The second sermon interweaves the perspectives of Bargaining Betty and Conceptualizing Charles. The third sermon appeals to all four perspectives.

Another way to practice your skills at using adult ways of knowing is to read each sermon through twice. The first time read it from the perspective for which it was written. Identify why this sermon would mean so much to that particular perspective. Then read it a second time, but now engage a different way of knowing. What might a listener who embodies that perspective find missing in the sermon? The goal of your two readings is not to conclude you liked or did not like the sermon. Instead, you are seeking to understand how the same sermon functions differently for people with different ways of knowing.

Here is a sermon on James 4:1-6 that speaks predominantly to the perspective of Affiliating Al. Sometimes it moves into other ways of knowing, but right from the start the sermon places a strong accent on interpersonal relations and how one feels. After reading the sermon from the perspective of Affiliating Al, read it from the perspective of Conceptualizing Charles, and then imagine the two of them having a conversation about the sermon afterward.

Sermon 1

Best friends.
They grew up as neighbors in Westfield, New Jersey.
They played on the same lacrosse team.
They served together in Korea as lieutenants in the U.S. Army.
They went to the same college and roomed together for four years.
They went on double dates together.
Their wives became good friends.
When they had kids, their families took vacations together.

Ed and Wally were the best of friends.
They knew everything about each other.
They were there for each other when tragedy came:
when Ed's father died . . .
when Wally's son was born with Down syndrome . . .
when Ed's wife was diagnosed with cancer . . .
when Wally lost his job.

They've been there for each other during the best of times, too.
They offered the toast as the best man at each other's wedding.
They celebrated with each other at the birth of each other's children.
They golfed together and they helped each other deal
with the joys and challenges of retirement.
It has been a lifelong friendship.

The best thing about this friendship
is that Ed and Wally really know each other.
They see things the same way and share the same outlook on life.
In fact, there is not a part of their lives
about which the other doesn't know.

They know how the other reacts and feels,
they know each other's goals and dreams.

They know each other's likes and dislikes.
They share the same values
of friendship,
of family,
of time spent with loved ones.
They have been loyal to each other.
They have kept confidences with each other,
they have kept their promises
and kept their word.
Ed and Wally have been faithful friends for decades.

It is not as though they haven't had their share
of problems and misunderstandings,
but they have stuck around to sort them out,
talk them through,
and move through miscommunication with honesty.

It has been a journey worth the effort.
For, when the days are over,
they each are thankful for each other,
thankful for a friend to golf with,
to cry with,
to share fears with,
and to just be with when there are no words.

Can we look at Ed and Wally's friendship
and think about our relationship with God?
There must be similarities.

No, we don't go golfing with God,
nor do we room together in college.
Friendship with God is certainly not *exactly* like a human friendship.
But there are similarities.

In this morning's text,
James talks about friendship with the world
and friendship with God.
He asks:
"Those conflicts and disputes among you? Where do they come
   from?"

According to James
they seem to be a manifestation of the conflict going on within us
between our own friendship with the world and our friendship with
   God.
But James says:
"Do you not know that friendship with the world is enmity with
   God?" (James 4:4)
According to James we cannot live two different lives.
Either we make friends with God or with the unjust world.

For those of the first century,
to be friends with one another
meant to see things the same way
and to share the same outlook.
So, to be friends of the world means, for James,
that one chooses to live by the logic of envy, rivalry, and violence.
But to be friends with God
is all about sharing a life with God who gives all the more grace
   (v. 6).

First of all, it is the shared values and loyalty
that are the foundation of any good friendship,
even our friendship with God.
Those values that God has, we must have.
Those values of unconditional love,
of justice and relationships with all of God's children,
of peace in people's lives

and peace among the nations.
And the values of compassion and kindness
offered without expectation of receiving the same in return.
Valuing who people *are*
instead of what they *have*
or what they *do* for a living.
Valuing the gifts of the Spirit in all of God's children
instead of the material gifts given with strings attached.
Values.
Shared values.
This is what solidifies a friendship and draws us together.
And this is what helps solidify our friendship with God.
Do we share God's values?

In addition to shared values, loyalty makes for a solid friendship.
God is loyal.
God's faithfulness is everlasting.
The psalmist sings with joy that "the steadfast love of the Lord never
  ceases."
Over and over again the Scriptures tell of God's loyalty.
What is important is *our* loyalty.
Our devotion.
Our commitment to the relationship.
Is our commitment to God of such importance that we will be a loyal
  friend?

James is writing to people like us,
people with whom God is not yet finished.
You see, James is writing to members of the Christian community
who gather in the name of Jesus
and profess their faith in the risen Christ,
but whose values and loyalty are not yet fully in line with God's.

It is hard to rid ourselves
of the envy and the competition and violence of the world,

since we live in the midst of it all.
But for James,
that is our goal,
that is our aim.
That is our desire when we seek to be friends with God.

James invites us to prayer
as the place where we can work on our friendship with God.
For in prayer we intimately encounter God,
whom we approach with complete honesty.
In prayer we strip away
all the things of the world that get in the way,
and we come into God's presence with our true selves,
our honest selves,
our whole heart.

When we develop a friendship with God,
in many ways it is like being friends with our college roommate.
God knows our dirty laundry,
and God knows where we throw it.
God knows the words we use even when no one is around.
God knows our ugly habits.
God knows our weaknesses and our internal desires.

But God also knows our dreams for the future,
our dreams for our friends and family,
and our desires and motivations in all of life.

James invites us, even today,
to turn to God intentionally and wholeheartedly.
If you have ever gotten to the end of the song and dance "The Hokey
    Pokey,"

you know what you are supposed to do at the end.
You know that after you put your head in and your right arm in and
    all that,
you are supposed to put your whole self in.

That's what the dance of friendship with God
has got to be about.
Putting your whole self in.
Not holding back.
Not holding back any part of who we are.
Then, and only then,
will we experience the grace that God has for us (v. 6).
Then, and only then, will we know the joy of friendship with God.

(Pause)

My dad had many friends,
but Wally was his closest.
My dad and Wally enjoyed many years of wonderful friendship.
My dad knew how to be a friend.
I have no doubt about this.
But as I look back,
I wonder if my dad had a friendship with God.
I wonder if my father knew how to "put his whole self in."
I wonder what kind of relationship my dad, Ed,
had with God.
I wonder.

Will your children wonder about you?
Will your grandchildren wonder?
Will your friends wonder?
What is your friendship with God like?
What part of your life are you holding back?

May it be that no one will have to wonder…[10]

This first sermon employs predominantly the perspective of Affiliating Al. But now we want to consider the blending of perspectives. The next sermon, based on Matthew 2:1-12, the journey of the magi to the Christ child, interweaves the perspectives of Bargaining Betty and Conceptualizing Charles. Read it first from their perspectives, then from the perspectives of Affiliating Al and Dialectical Donna. Once again your goal is not to conclude that the sermon is good or bad, but to understand more keenly why the same sermon, received and processed through different ways of knowing, has a greater or lesser impact. Since this involves juggling two perspectives at once, we have provided parenthetical comments to help you in your analysis. To show how the preacher is also adept at using the multiple intelligences that we explored in chapter 2, we have highlighted their use in **bold** type.

Because the sermon uses a clear story line, it is easy for any of the other adult perspectives to follow the preacher's flow of thought. The narrative structure (**Word Smart**) and the rhythmic refrain "never be the same again" (**Music Smart**) provides a "sermon trunk" that invites responses from other perspectives, including the child's perspective of Literal Larry as described in chapter 3.

Sermon 2

Have you ever experienced
Something that you were
Sure would change your life forever?[11]

Perhaps you remember
An event where you
Lost your innocence.
Perhaps you remember
The first time you gave your
Parents credit for actually
Knowing something.
Perhaps you remember

The first time you had
A friend or relative die.
Perhaps you remember the
First time you were involved
In the birth of a baby—
Either your own child,
Or a child of someone close to you.

From these experiences,
You would never be the same again.

(The list of possible experiences, each beginning with "perhaps" is both **Self Smart** and **People Smart**, and it acknowledges how Bargaining Betty focuses on diversity and interpersonal relationships. It is also **Logic Smart** and provides Conceptualizing Charles an opportunity to reflect analytically on life.)

From Matthew's Gospel,
We learn of some other people
Who were affected by a baby's
Birth and would never be the same again.

The scripture says that the baby
Named Jesus was born during
The reign of King Herod.

(Here begins a rehearsing of the narrative that uses **Picture** and **Body Smarts**. The mention of the "star" might evoke **Nature Smart**. The clarifications about who Herod is and how he acts provide coherence, a quality that is especially appealing to Conceptualizing Charles. Bargaining Betty will be alert to the description of King Herod's coercive rule since it contradicts her fundamental principle of not forcing one's will upon others.)

Now, King Herod was a tyrant
King who obsessed about the
Security of his rule.

He thwarted opposition by
Having people executed.
He took money from the rich
In order to serve as his revenue.
This revenue was used to pay off his debts and
Fund an army to keep security.
Herod felt that his security
Was being threatened
After he received news
From the magi
Who came and told him
They had seen a star
Rising for the newborn king of the Jews.
Scripture says he was disturbed by this news.
King Herod would never be the same again.

(The phrase "Scripture says" and citing the text represents the external absolute that is important to both Bargaining Betty and Affiliating Al. They want to hear what the Bible says, and the preacher tells them. The phrase "Scripture says" also provides Conceptualizing Charles a criterion for judging if the preacher's interpretation is valid. He will keenly follow the observation about Herod's fear for his security since this relates to his concerns about justice, power, and institutional structures.)

We read that Herod
Collects the chief priests and scribes
Of the Jews in order to
Figure out where this baby was born.

Bethlehem, they tell Herod.
These scribes and priests would
Never be the same again.

After speaking to the scribes and priests,
He summons the magi back to him.
Herod tells the magi to go to the child
To pay homage to him.
This is a devious plan.
He deceives the magi by claiming
His intentions are good.
The magi leave and follow the
Star to the house where the child
Lay sleeping.

(Deceptive behavior is an affront to Bargaining Betty's understanding of justice based on conventional images of good behavior and is severely critiqued by Conceptualizing Charles, who values legal rights and laws that provide for the maintenance of society.)

Scripture tells us that the magi
Were overjoyed even before
Entering the house where the baby was born.
What did they expect when they entered?
Why were they already happy?
What they saw inside would never
Let them be the same again.

They finally enter the house and see
Mary, the mother, and the baby.
They bow and pay homage to the
Baby and then present the baby with gifts.
These gifts were the stock-in-trade of the magi,
And the oils could be used to either

Anoint a king or anoint the dead.
Mary and Joseph accepted the gifts
On behalf of the child.
They would never be the same again.

After the presentation of the gifts,
We are told the magi go home
By another route because
They were warned in a dream
Not to go back to Herod.

Have you ever wondered what
Happened to these magi when
Herod discovered they
Did not return to him?

Does Herod have them killed?
How do the magi get the courage
To disobey one powerful king
For a child who was only rumored
To be a king?

This experience of seeing the star
And the mother
And the child
Would never let them be the same again.

(The following alternatives appeal to Bargaining Betty's awareness
of diversity because they permit choices based on one's preferences.
Conceptualizing Charles will think of valid criteria for making a
rational decision about the suggestions.)

How does the reading of this
Story each year affect you
And this whole congregation?

Are we willing to
Disobey or challenge those in power
Because we fear for the
Lives of helpless children?

Are we willing to go home
By an alternate route?
Maybe not a literal one, but a spiritual one.
This new route may take us by some
People we have never seen before—
The hungry, the homeless,
The very rich, the very poor,
Those with different ideas, beliefs, orientations,
And those with different skin color and abilities.

(Bargaining Betty will be glad for the multiple questions the preacher raises because they do not coerce the listeners into a single response. Conceptualizing Charles will appreciate the preacher's separating a symbol from the thing it represents when she asks about taking an alternate route: "Maybe not a literal one, but a spiritual one." The open-ended but probing questions are **Self** and **People Smart**.)

The magi went searching for whatever
The star was announcing.
But the story does not end
When they see the child.

No, the awesome part of this story
Comes when they choose
Not to support the one in power,
The status quo, the state king.

(Bargaining Betty might be relieved that the magi did not side with the coercive tyrant Herod. Conceptualizing Charles might consider the possible effects on society if people in the present day were to ignore what is commanded by political authorities.)

The magi listen to their dreams and take an alternate
Route home.
They would never be the same again.

Will we also listen to our dreams of how
This world might be different if we
Took an alternate route because of the
Birth of a child named Jesus?

I wonder if we would, or could, ever be the same again.[12]

(The sermon leaves the options open for Bargaining Betty who is
eager to answer the questions in light of her feelings, and for
Conceptualizing Charles who can bring his rational decision making
to what the preacher asks.)

Our final homily attempts to integrate all four adult ways of knowing.
It is based on the greatest commandment as recorded in Mark: "Jesus
answered, 'The first [commandment] is "Hear, O Israel: the Lord our God,
the Lord is one; you shall love the Lord your God with all your heart, and
with all your soul, and with all your mind, and with all your strength"'"
(Mark 12:29-30). The sermon also draws upon a verse from Paul: "Let the
same mind be in you that was in Christ Jesus" (Philippians 2:5).

The homily interprets for each of the four adult perspectives what it
means to love God "with all your mind." The preacher begins with a quotation from an interview with a child whose words we cited in chapter 3.
They exemplify the perspective of Magical Maggie. Although represent-
ing "the mind" of a young child, the girl's speech is so vivid and memo-
rable that it delights most adults no matter what their way of knowing.

The preacher connects the sermon together with the recurring phrase
"the mind of a child." Although the form of this homily may strike some
as rather unusual, it makes me (Tom) think of a conversation I had many
years ago with the homiletician Clement Welsh, who then taught at the
College of Preachers in Washington, D.C. He described a kind of sermon

outline to me that he called "the string of pearls." Each section has a distinct character and is somewhat independent of what precedes and follows. A repeated phrase—"the string"—holds it together, suggesting to the listeners that the different sections may be more interrelated than first strikes the mind. It is a homiletical pattern that comes close in spirit to what Gene Lowry terms "the conversational-episodal sermon."[13]

Sermon 3

"Air. God's everywhere."
That's what a four-year-old girl said
when she was asked what God might look like.
"Air. You know why? God's everywhere."
The mind of a child.

New Science physicists tell us
that subatomic electrons and photons
have both position and motion
at the same time.
They are both particles and waves.
But you can't see both position and motion
at the same time.
If you look for the particle,
then the wave will be invisible to you.
If you look for the wave,
then the particle will be invisible to you.
It's sort of like the creed,
"I believe in one God,
the Father Almighty,
maker of heaven and earth,
and of all things visible and invisible."

"Air. God's everywhere,"
in "all things visible and invisible."
The mind of a child.

(The images of waves and particles appeal especially to the analytical and reflective capacities of Conceptualizing Charles and Dialectical Donna. Although not foreign to the thinking of Affiliating Al and Bargaining Betty, the paradoxical characteristics—"both position and motion at the same time"—might be a challenge for these perspectives. However, they may find themselves bonding emotionally to the lines from the Nicene Creed, especially if that is a valued part of their tradition. Conceptualizing Charles might seek to explain the concepts of "visible and invisible" in terms of a rational thought. Dialectical Donna might find in the creed a vision of reality that encompasses but exceeds what humans know scientifically. The sermon has expanded the child's concept that "God's everywhere" to "all things visible and invisible.")

> New Science physicists tell us
> that paired electrons
> that move in opposite directions,
> one upward and one downward,
> can be separated from one another,
> even at great distances.
> And if they change the direction of one
> the other will change its direction too,
> even at great distances
> and without any visible or invisible
> exchange of energy
> They are just interrelated.
> They are just interconnected.
> And that's how all things are.
>
> "Air. God's everywhere,"
> in the connections and relationships
> that hold everything together.
> The mind of a child.

(The images of paired electrons will entice the thought processes of Conceptualizing Charles and Dialectical Donna, and challenge the understandings of Affiliating Al and Bargaining Betty. But both Al and Betty may welcome as an absolute or preferential truth the idea that everything is "interrelated" and "interconnected." Conceptualizing Charles understands the phenomenon of the paired electrons as something discovered by rational scientific method. For Dialectical Donna the scientific descriptions are apt to resonate with her integrated, paradoxical vision of the universe. The sermon has used the child's belief that "God's everywhere" to evoke the possibility of these highly varied adult interpretations.)

Once upon a time,
a Hasidic rabbi was approached
by a pious soul complaining
that certain Jews were
staying up all night playing cards. The rabbi said, "That's good.
They are learning great concentration
and becoming skilled at
remaining awake for long hours.
When they finally turn to God
see what excellent servants
they will make for God."
I suppose they could learn
how to pay attention,
how to be present, and
how to bear that kind of mindfulness
of God's presence in each event of ordinary life.

"Air. God's everywhere,"
even in the mindfulness of God's presence.
The mind of a child.

(All the adult perspectives would enjoy the story attributed to Martin Buber.[14] Affiliating Al would respond positively to the idea of becoming "excellent servants" for God, while Bargaining Betty would like the preacher's leaving room for other interpretations of the story by saying "I suppose." The idea of "mindfulness" might appeal to Conceptualizing Charles as a way of satisfying his search for ways to be coherent and consistent. Dialectical Donna might consider how to incorporate mindfulness into her processes of integrative thought. The sermon has now expanded the child's "God's everywhere" to include the concept of "mindfulness.")

One day long ago,
the missionary named Paul
was trying to settle problems
of division and diversity
within a congregation at Philippi
in northeastern Greece.
He asked them to be humble
and not conceited,
and most of all to
"let the same mind be in you
that was in Christ Jesus."
I wonder if he was asking them
to recognize that they were and could be
of the same mind as Jesus.
I also wonder if he imagined that
they were and could be
part of the mind of God.

"Air. God's everywhere,"
in that same mind that was in Christ Jesus.
The mind of a child.

(Affiliating Al and Bargaining Betty might focus on the good behaviors of humility and being like Christ. Conceptualizing Charles might seek clarification about what Paul actually meant by "the mind" of "Christ Jesus." Dialectical Donna might start thinking what it would mean for human beings to have the mind of Christ in light of the complexity of God. The child's "God's everywhere" now includes the mind of Christ Jesus.)

And that same mind
once spoke through Jesus
when little children
were brought to him. He said,
"Let the little children come to me,
and do not stop them,
for it is to such as these
that the kingdom of God belongs."

"Air. God's everywhere."
The mind of a child.[15]

(The conclusion appeals to conventional feelings of love for children and to virtues such as humility embraced by Affiliating Al and preferred by Bargaining Betty. Conceptualizing Charles seeks to interpret the meaning of the claim that the kingdom of God belongs to "such as these." Dialectical Donna will contemplate what it means for "the mind of a child" to be "the mind of God," and try to work it into her integrated vision of reality.)

The sermon brings us back to the theme with which our book opened: all of us for all of God. But now the things we have learned about theories of knowing illumine what it takes to move toward that lofty goal. It takes the mind of a child and the mind of our multiple adult perspectives. It takes a spirit of hospitality toward them all, a spirit of gratitude at the varied ways God has fashioned our processes of perceiving and responding. It takes a willingness to pray for grace to live the first commandment.

How to Put It All Together

The Gift to Be Simple

Opposites are sometimes the same reality in different modes. As we read in the concluding sermon of the last chapter:

Subatomic electrons and photons
have both position and motion
at the same time.
They are both particles and waves.
But you can't see both position and motion
at the same time.
If you look for the particle,
then the wave will be invisible to you.
If you look for the wave,
then the particle will be invisible to you.

What is true of the physical world can be true of the spiritual world as well: opposites are sometimes the same reality in different modes.

Consider, for example, simplicity and complexity. We typically think of them as opposites. Effective sermons are characterized by simplicity. If a sermon is too complex it loses most listeners. The congregation cannot successfully construct what Reuel Howe calls "the church's sermon."[1] By simplicity we do not mean being simplistic, reducing everything to the least common denominator or avoiding complicated issues. Instead, we mean what the hymn writer wrote:

> 'Tis the gift to be simple,
> 'tis the gift to be free,
> 'tis the gift to come down where you ought to be.
> And when we find ourselves in the place just right,
> It will be in the valley of love and delight.[2]

When preachers come down where they "ought to be," the living Word of God and the congregation's deepest needs and hopes converge in a pattern that gives meaning to their lives and empowers them to embody the gospel. There is an intensity of illumination that is clear and bright.

But the same hymn that celebrates simplicity also recognizes the complexity that brings it to birth:

> 'Tis the gift to have friends and a true friend to be,
> 'Tis the gift to think of others not to only think of "me,"
> And when we hear what others really think and really feel,
> Then we'll all live together with a love that is real.

The theory of multiple intelligences and the ways of knowing of children and adults reveal that hearing "what others really think and really feel" is a complex process. However, out of that complexity it is possible for us preachers to come down where we "ought to be" and "find ourselves [and our congregations!] in the place just right." Here is a summation of how the complexity can nurture the simplicity of effective preaching.

GENERATING THOUGHTS FOR A SERMON

Every preacher is sometimes stumped by a biblical text or a topic. The desk is filled with books that have been read, commentaries consulted, printouts from online resources, but none of it sparks a vital idea for a sermon. The preacher would do anything for one good generative thought. The preacher knows exactly what the poet means when he says:

Thought, I love thought.
But not the jaggling and twisting of already existent ideas.[3]

We get stuck in "the jaggling and twisting of already existent ideas" because we are using only one way of knowing. Our minds wear ruts in the same old path. We are not able to get a fresh slant on things. There is a helpful analogy from the world of extracting natural gas from deep wells. Geologists have discovered that often when a well appears to be empty, there is still a great deal of fuel in the ground, but the only way to get at it is to drill at a different angle.

The same is true of preachers: there is a sermon waiting to be born, but the only way to bring it forth is to use a different way of knowing. So if you are stumped by a text or a topic, try any or all of these strategies for getting unstuck.

• Review the different smarts derived from multiple intelligences theory (chapter 2). Systematically use each intelligence to interpret the text or address the topic.

• Consult the charts that summarize the perspectives of Magical Maggie and Literal Larry (chapter 3). Imagine a conversation with them about the text or the topic. How do they see and talk about it?

• Invite into your study the perspectives of Affiliating Al, Bargaining Betty, Conceptualizing Charles, and Dialectical Donna (chapter 4). Try telling each one of them in turn what the sermon is about in a manner that is easily accessible to their unique ways of knowing.

• Use the above methods with a sermon preparation group, asking them to honor the multiple ways of knowing.

Most of the time you will not have to try out every strategy. You will feel the breakthrough when you hit upon the way of knowing you need. Instead of "the jaggling and twisting of already existent ideas" you will experience again how extraordinarily rich thought can be:

> Thought is the welling up of unknown life into consciousness,
> Thought is the testing of statements on the touchstone of the
> conscience,
> Thought is gazing on to the face of life, and reading what can be read,
> Thought is pondering over experience, and coming to conclusion.
> Thought is not a trick, or an exercise, or a set of dodges,
> Thought is a man in his wholeness wholly attending.[4]

Thought is a woman in her wholeness wholly attending. Thought is a congregation in its wholeness wholly attending.

HOLY ATTENDING

"Wholly attending" is holy attending. It is holy because it uses the multiple ways of knowing that our holy God has given us. Holy attending is more than a method for making our preaching accessible to a greater variety of people. It is a way of living faithfully in a postmodern world. "Postmodern" is one of those trendy terms that means a myriad of things to different people in different contexts. But for our purposes here, we define postmodernism as a way of thought that looks with suspicion on established authority and that deconstructs systems of power and meaning. John McClure observes that in postmodernism "there are no center and no margins. We live in a context of radical difference, in which everyone is 'other' and no one is 'same.'"[5]

McClure wonders, "Is it possible to preach in a truly decentered way?" He answers the question in part by naming a number of collaborative and conversational models that homileticians have developed to deal with postmodernism, calling them "homiletics of welcome, through which a multitude of others are seated at the homiletic table, contributing to both brainstorming sermons and providing feedback."[6] We affirm "homiletics of welcome" but are eager for them to include multiple ways of knowing along with their other vital concerns such as culture, class, and race. If we are going to work with "a multitude of others," we will need to honor their different ways of knowing. Without this, we may practice cognitive imperialism, assuming that one way of knowing trumps all the others, believing that my way of knowing *is* the way of salvation.

Cognitive inclusivity—attending to all ways of knowing—defuses cognitive imperialism by reminding us that we are not saved by our knowledge but by faith. Seeing faith in the context of multiple intelligences and varied ways of knowing reveals that our relationship to God may develop in an astounding number of different forms in the course of our lives. Cognitive inclusivity also reinforces Paul's insight that the members of Christ's Body have different gifts. What holds the Body together is not that everyone knows the same thing in the same way, but that by the grace of Christ they trust in God.

Recentered in God

As with every gift God bestows upon us, there is always the possibility of using our way of knowing for distorted ends. Sin can warp any human capacity. But the Holy Spirit can also use a church's multiple ways of knowing to make us more faithful to Christ. We saw this, for example, in the story of Susan, the little girl who, after attending the Christmas pageant, worried if anyone was feeding baby Jesus. Her child's way of knowing awakens our adult ways of knowing to the need to feed the hungry.

There is no hierarchy of epistemologies here. The complementarity of the different ways of knowing draws the church away from the sin of neglecting the hungry.

Cognitive inclusivity is one answer to McClure's profound question, "Is it possible to preach in a truly decentered way?" Yes, it is. By attending to multiple ways of human knowing we honor the many perspectives that members of the church have on God, the church, and the world. Cognitive inclusivity allows us to honor the unique perspectives of others without forcing them to see things our way.

But it also does something more. Cognitive inclusivity makes it possible to preach in a recentered way. It recenters us in the one God who has gifted us with our different ways of knowing. God is the One in whom all perspectives converge. Bargaining Betty and Conceptualizing Charles meet at the manger to consider a question that makes sense to both their unique perspectives: "I wonder if we would, or could, ever be the same again."[7] The paradoxical phenomena of subatomic particles and a child's insight, "Air. God's everywhere," converge in the mind of Christ.[8] Cognitive inclusivity makes it possible to preach in a recentered way by drawing upon all our modes of knowing to focus on the love and knowledge of God as revealed through Christ.

Can we use every way of knowing in every sermon? No, and it is not necessary. Different settings, occasions, and pastoral needs require that we appeal to some intelligences and ways of knowing and not others. However, clergy who regularly review their preaching in light of multiple intelligences and the different ways of knowing among children and adults will frequently discover that it recenters them in God, who is the very reason for their preaching in the first place. Drawing upon the source of every good and perfect gift, their preaching will invite and empower us who receive their sermons to give all of us to all of God.

NOTES

1. All of Us for All of God

1. The phrase is not original with us. I (Tom) learned it from James B. Ashbrook, a former colleague who taught pastoral theology at Colgate Rochester Divinity School/Bexley Hall/Crozer Theological Seminary. Professor Ashbrook also had heard it elsewhere but was not certain of its precise origin.

2. We have used the slashed translation "wind/spirit" because the word in Greek means both.

3. Quoted by Stephen H. Webb, *The Divine Voice: Christian Proclamation and the Theology of Sound* (Grand Rapids: Brazos, 2004), 93.

4. John Calvin, Institutes of the Christian Religion as printed in Richard Lischer, ed., *The Company of Preaching: Wisdom on Preaching, Augustine to the Present* (Grand Rapids: William B. Eerdmans, 2002), 364.

5. John S. McClure, *Otherwise Preaching: A Postmodern Ethic for Homiletics* (St. Louis: Chalice Press, 2001), 146.

6. Howard Gardner, *Frames of Mind: The Theory of Multiple Intelligences* (New York: Basic Books, 1993); *Multiple Intelligences: The Theory in Practice* (New York: Basic Books, 1993); *Intelligence Reframed: Multiple Intelligences for the 21st Century* (New York: Basic Books, 1999).

7. For example, James W. Fowler, *Stages of Faith: The Psychology of Human Development and the Quest for Meaning* (New York: Harper & Row, 1981); Mary M. Wilcox, *Developmental Journey: A Guide to the Development of Logical and Moral Reasoning and Social Perspective* (Nashville: Abingdon, 1979); and literature cited in H. Edward Everding, Jr., Mary M. Wilcox, Lucinda A. Huffaker, and Clarence H. Snelling Jr., *View Points: Perspectives of Faith and Christian Nurture* (Harrisburg, Pa.: Trinity Press International, 1998).

8. James R. Nieman and Thomas G. Rogers, *Preaching to Every Pew: Cross-Cultural Strategies* (Minneapolis: Fortress, 2001), 13.

9. McClure, *Otherwise Preaching*, 7.

10. Fred B. Craddock, *Preaching* (Nashville: Abingdon, 1985), 26–27.

11. Gregory the Great, "Catalogue of Hearers," in Lischer, ed., *The Company of Preaching*. The quotation is from the editor's introduction to Gregory the Great, 355.

12. Ibid., 356.

13. Ibid.

14. John S. McClure, *Preaching Words: 144 Key Terms in Homiletics* (Louisville: Westminster John Knox, 2007), 17.

15. Nieman and Rogers, *Preaching to Every Pew*, 16.

16. Ibid., 1.

17. For a brief discussion of the principle of all of us for all of God that uses cultural analysis rather than theories of learning and knowing see Thomas H. Troeger, *Preaching and Worship* (St. Louis: Chalice Press, 2003), 21–22.

18. Howard Gardner, *Frames of Mind: The Theory of Multiple Intelligences*, 10th Anniversary Edition (New York: Basic Books, 1993), 30.

19. Ibid., 57.

20. McClure, *Otherwise Preaching*, 134.

21. McClure, *Preaching Words*, 74. McClure is referring to and summarizing a Lilly-funded project led by Ronald J. Allen whose results are published by Chalice Press in four volumes and many articles.

22. O. C. Edwards, *A History of Preaching* (Nashville: Abingdon, 2004), 12.

23. Lucy Lind Hogan, *Graceful Speech: An Invitation to Preaching* (Louisville: Westminster John Knox, 2006), 20.

24. Ibid.

25. Ibid., 21.

26. All the letters are quoted from the letters to the editor in the *New York Times*, March 19, 2006, one week after the publication of Zizek's essay.

27. Saint Augustine, *Teaching Christianity: De Doctrina Christiana*, trans. Edmund Hill, O. P. (Hyde Park, N.Y.: New City Press, 2003), 124.

28. Ibid.

29. Paul Scott Wilson, *Preaching and Homiletical Theory* (St. Louis: Chalice Press, 2004), 55.

30. Thomas H. Troeger, *Borrowed Light: Hymn Texts, Prayers, and Poems* (New York: Oxford University Press, 1994), 132.

2. Multiple Intelligences

1. For a concise discussion and bibliography on authenticity as "the modern ideal among preachers of being true to oneself" see McClure, *Preaching Words*, 5–6.

2. Reuel L. Howe, *Partners in Preaching: Clergy and Laity in Dialogue* (New York: Seabury, 1967). We are very indebted to Howe's work for its fine insights about the nature of communication between preacher and congregation. But since it was written in the 1960s some of the examples and concerns now seem dated so we are using his basic principles but restating them for our time.

3. Ibid., 72.

4. Ibid., 73.

5. Ibid., 61.

6. Ibid.

7. Ibid., 51–52.

8. We are moved by Kathy Black's significant work on the inadequacy of talking about only "hearing" a sermon when many people are deaf or hearing impaired. That is in part why we often use the phrase "receiving, processing and responding to a sermon." It allows for senses other than hearing. Nevertheless, we find the words "hearing" and "hearers" such a part of the idiom of homiletics that we will sometimes use them, but try to balance our use of hearing with other ways of talking about the congregation's participation in the

act of preaching. MI theory is hospitable to Black's insights because it honors multiple ways of processing reality. See Kathy Black, *A Healing Homiletic: Preaching and Disability* (Nashville: Abingdon, 1996).

9. For a creative critique of IQ theory see David Perkins, *Outsmarting IQ: The Emerging Science of Learnable Intelligence* (New York: The Free Press, 1995).

10. Elizabeth Barrett Browning, http://www.netpoets.com/classic/poems/008003.htm.

11. Howard Gardner, *Intelligence Reframed* (New York: Basic Books, 1999); see also Gardner, *Frames of Mind: The Theory of Multiple Intelligences* and *Multiple Intelligences: The Theory in Practice*.

12. Gardner, *Intelligence Reframed*, 33–34.

13. Ibid., 32.

14. Ibid., 53–77.

15. Ibid., 41.

16. Ibid., 42.

17. Ibid.

18. Ibid.

19. Ibid.

20. Ibid, 43.

21. Ibid.

22. Ibid, 48.

23. See, for example, Charles L. Bartow, *The Preaching Moment: A Guide to Sermon Delivery* (Nashville: Abingdon, 1980); G. Robert Jacks, *Getting the Word Across: Speech Communication for Pastors and Lay Leaders* (Grand Rapids: William B. Eerdmans, 1987); Henry Mitchell, *Celebration and Experience in Preaching* (Nashville: Abingdon, 1990); Thomas H. Troeger, *Ten Strategies for Preaching in a Multi Media Culture* (Nashville: Abingdon, 1996); Richard Ward, *Speaking from the Heart: Preaching with Passion* (St. Louis: Chalice Press, 2001). For a seminal theoretical work that has influenced these and many other homileticians who write about the orality of preaching see Walter Ong, *The Presence of the Word: Some Prolegomena for Cultural and Religious History* (New Haven, Conn.: Yale University Press, 1967).

24. I also illustrate how this method can result in a delivery that is more engaging for our media-saturated world. See Troeger, *Ten Strategies for Preaching in a Multi Media Culture*, 18–19.

25. Helpful tools for the analysis of a congregation's "language" can be found in James Hopewell, *Congregation: Stories and Structures* (Minneapolis: Augsburg Fortress, 1987). Leonora Tubbs Tisdale, *Preaching as Local Theology and Folk Art* (Minneapolis: Fortress, 1997).

26. For a fascinating discussion of the interplay of rhetoric and Christianity see Averil Cameron, *Christianity and the Rhetoric of Empire: The Development of Christian Discourse* (Berkeley: University of California Press, 1991).

27. McClure, *Preaching Words*, 54.

28. Ibid., 55.

29. From an unpublished sermon preached by Tim McLemore at Kesssler Park United Methodist Church, Dallas, Texas, on July 18, 2004.

30. John L. Bell, *The Singing Thing: A Case for Congregational Song* (Chicago: GIA Publications, 2000), 97.

31. Stephen H. Webb, *The Divine Voice: Christian Proclamation and the Theology of Sound* (Grand Rapids: Brazos, 2004), 27.

32. For a more elaborate treatment of this theme, see "Listen to the Music of Speech" in Thomas H. Troeger, *Imagining a Sermon* (Nashville: Abingdon, 1990), 67–88.

33. I (Tom) am indebted to Gwyn Walters, a Welsh preacher and homiletician, who lectured on the preacher's "tune" many years ago in the Academy of Homiletics.

34. McClure, *Preaching Words*, 63–64.

35. Charles Bugg as quoted by Mitties McDonald de Champlain, "What to Do while Preaching" in John S. McClure, ed., *Best Advice for Preaching* (Minneapolis: Fortress, 1998), 105.

36. We are indebted here to Richard Ward, *Speaking of the Holy: The Art of Communication in Preaching* (St. Louis: Chalice, 2001). We had several conversations with the author about these matters while he was writing his book.

37. Mitties McDonald de Champlain, "What to Do while Preaching" in McClure, ed., *Best Advice for Preaching*, 99–100.

38. Ibid., 111–12. De Champlain's chapter is filled with sound, practical advice on how to embody a sermon in a style congruent with the message and appropriate to one's natural way of being and the expectation of the congregation.

39. This spatial approach to the gospel story was first suggested to me (Tom) years ago when I attended a creative Bible study led by Walter Wink. He subsequently wrote a book on his methods: Walter Wink, *Transforming Bible Study: A Leader's Guide* (Nashville: Abingdon, 1980).

40. Mitchell, *Celebration and Experience in Preaching*, 89.

41. To examine indirect communication as a homiletical strategy see Fred Craddock, *Overhearing the Gospel* (Nashville: Abingdon, 1995).

42. For an excellent short monograph on the use of the self in preaching see Richard Thulin, *The I of the Sermon* (Eugene, Oreg.: Wipf & Stock, 2004).

43. George Arthur Buttrick, ed., *The Interpreter's Dictionary of the Bible: An Illustrated Encyclopedia*, vol. 4 (Nashville: Abingdon, 1962), 102.

44. For a wise and witty discussion about congregational responses to sermons and some very usable questions for guiding the discussion see David Schlafer, *Surviving the Sermon: A Guide for Those Who Have to Listen* (Boston: Crowley Publications, 1992). For clear yet sophisticated advice for preachers seeking to be effective in multicultural and multiethnic congregations see Nieman and Rogers, *Preaching to Every Pew*, 139–57.

45. We have adapted this exercise from Thomas Armstrong, *Multiple Intelligences in the Classroom*, 2nd ed. (Alexandria, Va.: Association for Supervision and Curriculum Development, 2000), 31–33.

46. Mitchell, *Celebration and Experience in Preaching*, 21–23.

47. Thomas Armstrong explores eight ways of teaching any subject in *Multiple Intelligences in the Classroom*. Christian educator Barbara Bruce provides similar guidance in two books developed before Gardner introduced naturalist intelligence: *7 Ways of Teaching the Bible to Children* (Nashville: Abingdon, 1996); *7 Ways of Teaching the Bible to Adults* (Nashville: Abingdon, 2000).

3. Preaching and Children's Ways of Knowing

1. Isaiah 11:6.

2. We use naive to describe a respected way of knowing that has not yet developed capacities for formal operations and critical thinking. In fact, through life experience this

naive capacity can be integrated with other cognitive capacities to form what Karl Barth and Paul Ricoeur describe as the second naiveté. For example, see Mark I. Wallace, *The Second Naiveté: Barth, Ricoeur, and the New Yale Theology*, Studies in American Biblical Hermeneutics 6 (Macon, Ga.: Mercer University Press, 1990; reissued with new introduction, 1995).

3. Carolyn C. Brown, *You Can Preach to the Kids Too! Designing Sermons for Adults and Children* (Nashville: Abingdon, 1997), 8.

4. Clark M. Williamson and Ronald Allen, *The Teaching Minister* (Louisville: Westminster John Knox, 1991), 84.

5. Thomas H. Troeger, *Above the Moon Earth Rises: Hymn Texts, Anthems, and Poems for a New Creation* (New York: Oxford University Press, 2002), 59–61.

6. I (Ed) conducted this interview with Henry in 1973. He was killed by a rock fall in the Patagonia National Park in 2005.

7. I (Ed) conducted this interview with Henry in 1978.

8. For a rationale to present these cognitive capacities as a typology and not hierarchical stages, see Everding, Wilcox, Huffaker, and Snelling, *View Points,* 13.

9. These descriptions are informed by Fowler, *Stages of Faith*; Sara Covin Juengst, *Sharing Faith with Children: Rethinking the Children's Sermon* (Louisville: Westminster John Knox, 1994); and Mary M. Wilcox, *Developmental Journey: A Guide to the Development of Logical and Moral Reasoning and Social Perspective* (Nashville: Abingdon, 1979).

10. The responses were first reported in H. Edward Everding Jr. and Mary M. Wilcox, "Kohlberg's Theory of Moral Reasoning for Biblical Interpretation," presented at the Annual Meeting of the Association of Professors and Researchers in Religious Education, November 1975. They were later utilized in Wilcox, *Developmental Journey.*

11. This is abstracted from an interview with a 4-and-1/2-year-old girl cited in Jim Fowler: "Life/Faith Patterns: Structures of Trust and Loyalty" in Jim Fowler and Sam Keen, *Life Maps: Conversations on the Journey of Faith*, ed. Jerome Berryman (Waco, Tex.: Word Books, 1978), 46.

12. This is taken from an interview done by Ed with Henry in 1973.

13. Eugene L. Lowry, *How to Preach a Parable: Designs for Narrative Sermons* (Nashville: Abingdon, 1989), 23.

14. Although the sermon was preached to a congregation, I (Tom) later worked it into a paper for an academic meeting: Thomas H. Troeger, "A Little Child Shall Lead Them: Parabolic Preaching as Recovery of the Child's Perceptive Capacities," The Academy of Homiletics, Papers of the Annual Meeting, Denver, Colo., 1999, 83–94. I (Ed) wrote a companion paper analyzing parables in light of theories of knowing: H. Edward Everding Jr., "Parables: Multiple Interpretations," The Academy of Homiletics, Papers of the Annual Meeting, Denver, Colo., 1999, 54. We are drawing upon both of those papers in this chapter.

15. David Curzon, ed., *Modern Poems on the Bible: An Anthology* (Philadelphia: The Jewish Publication Society, 1994), 7. Curzon's introduction is a lively and lucid essay about midrashim.

16. Brown, *You Can Preach to the Kids Too!*, 8.

4. Preaching and Adult Ways of Knowing

1. Buttrick, *Homiletic*, 61. The italics are Buttrick's.

2. For an extensive discussion of these perspectives see Everding, Wilcox, Huffaker, and Snelling, *View Points*.

3. Buttrick, *Homiletic*, 61–62. The italics are Buttrick's.

4. Ibid., 295.

5. Ibid., 296. The italics are Buttrick's.

6. Ibid.

7. McClure, *Otherwise Preaching*, 60.

8. Ibid., 68–69. Chapter 4 of this book, "Exiting the House of Reason: To the New Homiletic and Beyond," traces developments in our understanding of the nature and function of reason in homiletics. It makes a fine theological/philosophical complement to the way we are looking at adult ways of knowing in light of learning theory.

9. For a discussion of this very important distinction between position and pattern or content (of statement) and structure (of reasoning) see Everding, Wilcox, Huffaker, and Snelling, *View Points*, 18–20.

10. The sermon was preached by Victoria M. Isaacs.

11. This preacher likes to capitalize the first letter in each line when using the oral/aural style, and we have left the manuscript as she wrote it. Her method carries on a poetic convention that was common into the twentieth century.

12. The sermon was preached by Kimberly Dickerson.

13. Eugene L. Lowry, *The Sermon: Dancing the Edge of Mystery* (Nashville: Abingdon, 1997), 28.

14. The story is cited by Belden C. Lane, "Stalking the Snow Leopard: A Reflection on Work," *Christian Century* 101, no. 1 (January 4–11, 1984): 15.

15. The sermon was preached by Ed Everding.

5. How to Put It All Together

1. For a definition and discussion of this term see p. 24.

2. "Simple Gifts" was written by Shaker Elder Joseph Brackett Jr. in 1848. It was first published in *The Gift to Be Simple: Shaker Rituals and Songs*. The text of the hymn and this endnote are from http://www2.gol.com/users/quakers/simple_gifts.htm.

3. D. H. Lawrence, "Thought" in Christopher Ricks, *The Oxford Book of English Verse* (New York: Oxford University Press, 1999), 549.

4. Ibid.

5. McClure, *Preaching Words*, 113.

6. Ibid.

7. See the next to the last sermon in chapter 4.

8. See the last sermon in chapter 4.